Drinking and Driving

Janet Grosshandler

ROSEN PUBLISHING GROUP, INC./NEW YORK

Published in 1990 by The Rosen Publishing Group, Inc.
29 East 21st Street, New York, NY 10010

First Edition

Library of Congress Cataloging-In-Publication Data

Grosshandler, Janet
Coping with drinking and driving / Janet Grosshandler.—1st ed.
p. cm.
Includes bibliographical references.
Summary: Discusses the effects and dangers involved in combining drinking with driving, the legal implications, and various methods of fighting the problem.
ISBN 0-8239-1156-X
1. Drinking and traffic accidents—United States—Juvenile literature. [1. Drinking and traffic accidents. 2. Drunk driving.] I. Title
HE5620.D7G76 1990
363.12′57—dc20 89-77060
CIP
AC

Manufactured in the United States of America

For Nate, Jeff, & Mike,
and Edna Holstein, my mother.
And always for Hank.

ABOUT THE AUTHOR ◇

Janet Grosshandler is a guidance counselor at Jackson Memorial High School, Jackson, New Jersey. Helping teenagers work through difficult problems in their lives has been a high priority in her life.

Janet earned a BA at Trenton State College in New Jersey and followed soon after with an MEd from Trenton while teaching seventh-grade English. Working as a guidance counselor for thirteen years has given her a wide range of experience with adolescents. She also writes a weekly newspaper column, "Counselor's Corner," which gives advice to teens and their parents on coping with the ups and downs of the teenage years.

Recently widowed, Janet lives in Jackson with her three young sons, Nathan, Jeff, and Michael. She squeezes in time for running, coaching soccer and Little League, and reading.

Acknowledgments

Many thanks are due to people who eased my way in writing this book.

To my sons, Nate, Jeff, and Mike, who gave up their time on the computer for Mom to finish this book—you always are proud of me and I of you.

To my mother, Edna Holstein, without whom I could never have accomplished all that I have so far, my thanks and my love.

To Ruth Rosen, who understood and supported me through some difficult times.

To Vickie Wilson—thanks for the tons of material, information, and contacts.

My thanks and appreciation to all the teenagers who share their lives with me so that I can understand their realities and their problems. I learn from you every day.

And it's important for me to mention here my husband, Hank, who died on April 28, 1989, of cancer. He made my life special and wonderful. I am what I am today because of his unconditional love and total support.

Some of the names in this book have been changed to protect the anonymity of the teenagers who were interviewed. A few are composite stories of two or three teens.

Contents

Opinion Survey

Directions: To indicate your feelings about each statement accurately, mark the following in the blanks:

D—strongly disagree
d—moderately disagree
?—unsure
a—moderately agree
A—strongly agree.

1. Driving home from a party after you've been drinking is very dangerous. ____
2. Some people drive more cautiously after they've been drinking. ____
3. If someone you hardly know at a party wants to drive drunk, it's really none of your business. ____
4. Teenagers have more accidents after drinking than adults. ____
5. Alcohol starts affecting you as soon as it is swallowed. ____
6. The odds of being in an alcohol-related accident in your life are very small. ____
7. Teens convicted of drunk driving should receive less severe punishment than adult offenders. ____
8. Fifty percent of fatal traffic accidents involve alcohol. ____

9. A few wine coolers can't make you drunk enough to have difficulty driving. ____
10. Alcohol is absorbed into your bloodstream very slowly. ____
11. Drinking two cups of strong coffee can sober you up enough to drive safely after drinking. ____
12. When you drink two 12-ounce cans of beer, it takes one hour for the alcohol to leave your body so it is safe to drive. ____
13. The chances of being caught driving drunk are small enough that it's okay to be a little high when you are behind the wheel. ____
14. The advertisements of alcohol and beer companies are harmless and don't really influence teens to drink. ____
15. The alcohol of choice for most teenagers is beer. ____
16. Most police officers will let you off with a warning if they stop you for driving while intoxicated, especially if it is your first time. ____
17. Judges go easy on teen first-time offenders for drunk driving. ____
18. Some drivers drive better after a few drinks. ____
19. It takes a lot of drinks for the alcohol level in your blood to reach .10, the legal limit for intoxicated drivers. ____

CHAPTER ◇ 1

Robbie's Story

"Happy birthday, sweetheart," Mother said to me the morning of my eighteenth birthday.

My father grinned and jangled car keys in front of my eyes.

"All right!" I grabbed the keys and scooped up my gym bag, ready to take off for school. "Thank you! Thank you!" I called to my parents over my shoulder as I raced out to my very own car.

The old Chevy pick-up truck had been my father's, but it became mine on my eighteenth birthday. It's all mine now! Freedom!

Mom and Dad came out on the front porch as I revved the engine. "Drive carefully!" I heard them call as I threw them a wave out the window and took off down our quiet street en route to pick up my girlfriend.

"Oh Robbie, it's finally yours! I love it! Now we can go anywhere we want to!" Betsy said as she climbed in. All the way to school we talked about how we would change some of the inside of the pick-up to make it really mine, really ours.

"Where are we going tonight?" Betsy asked.

"First we have to spend some time with my folks. I owe them for giving me Dad's car. After that we're on our own. PARRRRRTY!" We laughed with glee, and the sense of elation over being eighteen and totally grown-up ricocheted in my car. MY CAR. Man, this was the greatest!

"Now listen, young man," Mom gave me a stern look. "If having your own car makes you drive the way you peeled out of here this morning, I may ask for the keys back."

"No way, Mom! You don't have to worry about me. I know what I'm doing." I gave her a hug to reassure her, because my mother sometimes follows up on her threats. "Besides," I hugged the keys to my chest, "you'll have to kill me to get these away from me now!"

"Very funny," she said with a worried look on her face.

"Ease up, Judy," my father joined us. "He's got a good head on his shoulders. Here, son." Dad handed me a glass of champagne.

"A toast to my grown-up son on his eighteenth birthday," he said. "Here's to good luck and good fortune through graduation and on to the university."

"Hear, hear," Mom joined in.

We all clinked glasses and shared the warmth of the moment. I felt I really was an adult now in their eyes.

"What about me?" My kid sister, Debbie, held up an empty juice glass. "Don't I get to join in this celebration, or are you leaving me out of this too?" I think she really meant that last part, although she gave a little smile.

"Why not?" Dad poured her some champagne.

She gulped it down. "Maybe I'll see you at Johnston's party later," she said to me.

"No way. His party's for high school kids, not eighth-graders."

"Well, I might just show up with Tommy Samuels."

"He's seventeen! What are you doing with him?"

"He asked me out. So there! And I'm going. If you don't like it, don't go."

Jeez, Ricky Johnston was kind of giving this party for me and Betsy. I didn't want my kid sister around to ruin it. "Just stay out of my way."

"I will."

Debbie had been really grouchy lately. Up and down moodwise. But I didn't have time to worry about her. I had more important things to do tonight!

Ricky's party turned out to be a blast! Wall-to-wall kids and two kegs of beer. After the champagne at home and some of that cold keg beer, I was feeling no pain. I was having such a good time that I hardly noticed Debbie. I figured she could handle herself; I wasn't going to be her keeper and count how many times she went back to the keg.

Everyone made a fuss about my birthday like it was a big deal. I think the other kids just wanted more reasons to celebrate. A few girls came over and gave me some very sexy birthday kisses. I could tell that Betsy was getting annoyed, but I didn't care. Betsy loved me. These girls liked me. I was the hit of the party. I could do nothing wrong. Tonight was my night!

"Come on, Babe, let's go," I whispered to Betsy about one o'clock. I had a surprise hidden in the pick-up for her.

"Don't you want to ask Cindy and Laura too, Rob? They've been hanging on you all night." She was drunker than I had thought. "You can have all three of us tonight. How about that?" Betsy emptied her last drop of beer and threw the cup on Ricky's kitchen floor.

Shoot. I wanted tonight to be perfect. Now I had to sweet-talk Betsy out of her mood.

"I have something in my car for you, and only you." I kissed her ear the way she liked it. It didn't take too much convincing. Betsy was pretty high, and I could tell she was getting in a sexy mood. That was fine with me. That's what I had had in mind for later anyway.

POP! The cork exploded off the bottle of champagne I had taken from home. It bounced off the roof of the pick-up.

"I forgot cups."

Betsy took the bottle from my hands. "That's okay. We can share the bottle. We share germs anyway." She giggled and gave me a sloppy kiss after taking a swig.

We snuggled down to an hour of kissing and drinking, feeling very mellow. Finishing the champagne really turned us on, and we forgot the time as we got more involved with each other.

"Oh, man! It's almost three! My parents will kill me." Betsy struggled up, shaking her head to clear it.

I didn't want to go either, but staying out after Betsy's curfew too often got us separated for a weekend. I put the pick-up in gear and took off.

Trusty pick-up. It buzzed along nice and smooth. I was buzzed too, but I knew I was okay to drive. This was my night! Nothing could stop me!

Oh *God*! I don't know how it happened! It must have been icy on that curve or something. The pick-up skidded out of control. I knew Betsy and I would be all right. It was a heavy car, wasn't it? I didn't have time to think anymore. The last thing I heard was Betsy screaming and screaming as we slammed into the telephone pole.

I felt the terrible jolt as we crashed. Glass shattered as Betsy went headfirst through the windshield. I tried to yell her name, but the pain in my chest and head were excruciating. "Betsy!"

When I woke up, everything was calm and quiet. Police and first-aid people were running all over, but I couldn't hear them. What was going on? Was I deaf or something?

A policeman was bending over Betsy, who was lying on the hood of the truck. I saw him shake his head and try to find a pulse on her. Then I looked carefully at my girl. Oh, Bets, I'm so sorry.

The side of her face was shredded and bleeding. One eye was out of its socket. Blood poured from where her eye used to be. Her mouth was open as if she had never finished that last scream.

They lifted my sweet Betsy onto an ambulance stretcher, covering her broken body and bleeding face with a blanket. I knew Betsy was dead, but I felt numb, so numb that I couldn't talk.

What was wrong with me? I couldn't hear. I couldn't talk. Why weren't the policemen racing around to help me? I looked down at my body. I was crumpled under the steering wheel, wedged between the crushed door and the seat. Glass was shattered all over me. I couldn't feel anything. Oh, God. Help me!

They finally got me out of the car and put me on a stretcher next to Betsy. Hey, wait a minute! Don't pull that blanket over my head too! I didn't die? Did I? I'm not dead! I just turned eighteen. I'm graduating in a few months. I already sent my money to the university.

I can't be dead! I haven't finished living yet!

It was dark and cold in the drawer. I watched as my parents came in to identify me. I don't want you to see me like this. Oh, Mom, don't cry. I didn't mean to do this. Dad, it was an accident. I tried to be careful. Really. This was my night, remember? Nothing could stop me.

My funeral was the pits. My parents and kid sister cried

and cried. I wanted to tell them that I loved them. When was the last time I had done that?

My two best friends stayed with my family the whole time. Richie, Fitz, you big jerks. You're supposed to be strong. You're out of control. I never knew you'd be like this.

Betsy's parents didn't come. I guess Betsy was someplace else. Oh, Bets, I'm sorry. We were supposed to have a good time, not die. I don't want you to hate me for eternity for driving when I was drunk like that.

No! Don't put me in that cold, dark ground. This is a mistake. It must be. I didn't play the last basketball game. Coach will be mad at me. I still have to hand in my history term paper. It's only half done, still sitting in my typewriter.

I can't be dead. Please, God, all I ask is one more chance. I'll be careful and I'll never drink and drive again. One more chance, please?

I can't be dead. I'm only eighteen.

CHAPTER ◇ 2

Overview, Research, and Statistics

FACT: In America, over 1 *million* people suffer crippling and other serious injuries every year because of drunk drivers.

FACT: Every driver has a 50 percent chance of being in an alcohol-related car crash in his or her lifetime. That's one out of every two Americans.

FACT: Young people (ages sixteen to twenty-four) cause 44 percent of drunk driving accidents. The same age group comprises only 22 percent of drivers.

FACT: One American life is lost every 23 *minutes* in alcohol-related car crashes.

FACT: Drunk drivers cause more deaths, injuries, and destruction than muggers, rapists, and thieves.

American teenagers are killing themselves at an alarming rate in car crashes. These accidents usually happen on a Friday or Saturday night and many times involve a teenage driver who has been drinking.

LEADING CAUSES OF DEATHS OF TEENAGERS

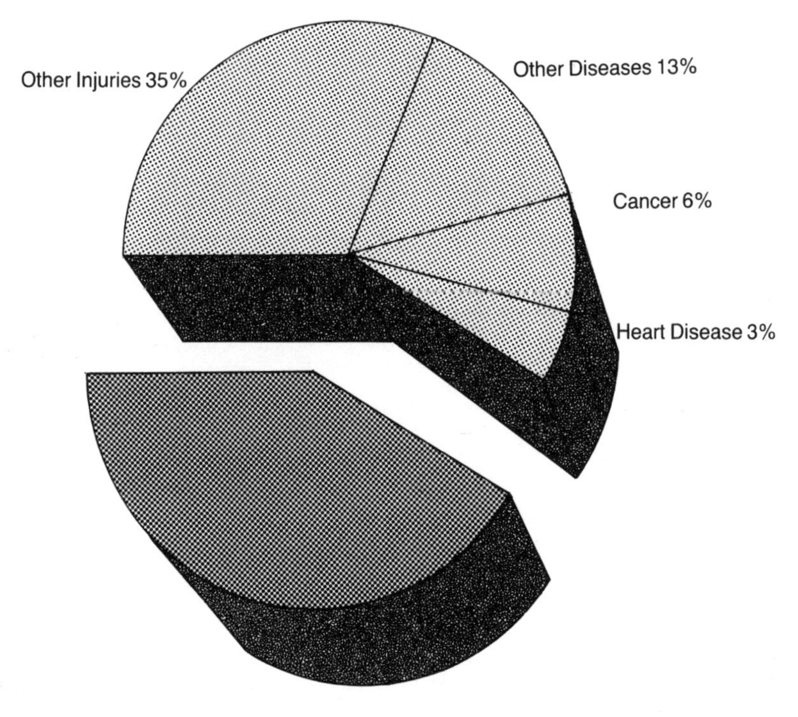

Reprinted by permission of Insurance Institute for Highway Safety

Sources: National Highway Traffic Safety Administration, Mothers Against Drunk Driving (MADD).

"There's nothing much to do around here, so we go over to Jason's house and drink on Friday and Saturday nights."

FACT: Over 90 percent of high school seniors and over 50 percent of seventh-graders have tried alcohol.

"Beer's easiest to get. We just take it from home, or somebody's older brother or sister gets it for us. My friend is lucky. His parents buy it for him."

FACT: The most popular drink among teenagers is beer.

"It's the thing to do around here. How else can we have fun?"

FACT: On the average, teenagers drink about five times a month.

"I can handle it. I don't have a drinking problem. We just do it because it makes us feel good."

FACT: There are an estimated 3.3 million problem drinkers among teenagers ages fourteen to seventeen.

Children and teenagers are bombarded with "Drinking is fun" messages from the media. You can't have "fun" unless you "party," and you can't "party" unless you drink. Getting "wasted" is the goal of many a teenager's weekend plans.

Spuds McKenzie, the "party animal," has become a best-selling stuffed toy for children. Kids get the message that "Drinking is great. Everyone should do it," as they cuddle their Spuds doll.

Teens today have "nothing to do" except drink and hang out. It has become their recreation of choice. Why are the school dances empty? Why are the stands at basketball games vacant? Even if the kids go bowling, they drink first to feel "good." Why can't kids have fun without drinking?

True, peer pressure is great. It's cool to drink and get wasted. It's not cool to refuse a beer, saying, "No, thanks. I don't need that for a good time."

Look around at a family gathering on Thanksgiving or another holiday. Divide your family in two, half on the left side of the room and half on the right. Look at all the faces of people you love on one of those sides. One half of your family can expect to be in an alcohol-related car crash at least once in their lifetime. For a few of them, it will be the last accident they'll ever be in.

When you get in a car, your chances of being in an accident are one in seven. When you get in a car slightly drunk or with a drunk driver, your chances drop to one in three. Are those the kinds of odds you want to bet your life on?

Eighty percent of fatal accidents are first accidents, and the scariest statistics show that teenage drivers are at great risk. Too many teens and young adults kill themselves or others because they mix booze and cars.

Usually a common explanation for this consistent involvement of teen drivers in accidents is their inexperience with driving and with drinking and driving.

* * *

"I'm okay to drive. I only had a six-pack."

"I'm not stupid. I didn't have that much to drink."

"I drive better when I'm drunk."

It takes very little to prove these statements false. You may say, "If I drink and drive, that's *my* problem."

No, it is not. It is *everybody's* problem.

Imagine driving with your girlfriend after you've partied to the "feeling no pain" stage. *Look out*! You didn't see that red light! Your girlfriend crashes head first through the windshield, landing on the hood of your car.

Think about picking up your little brother after his soccer game when you've been chugging a few beers at your friend's house. You're late, so you drive a little faster because your judgment is impaired. *Watch out for that curve! You're going too fast*! The side of your car that gets wrapped around the tree is where your little brother was sitting.

How do you face your parents? How do you face yourself? If you make it out of that wreck alive...

Sure, this is strong stuff. It's also true stuff. Very real, horrible, sad, deadly stuff. And it happens every 23 minutes.

Not me, you say.

Yes, you. Yes, everyone.

In this country, the average age at which kids begin to drink is thirteen and moving younger every year. It used to be that the greatest proportion of teenage drinkers were boys, but girls are now drinking on a more even keel with them. If there are over 3.3 *million* teenage problem drinkers, could you look around the lunchroom at your school and pick them out?

Probably you could name a few. And possibly you have

suspicions about a few more. But many young drinkers hide very well the fact that they drink. They may steal their liquor from home or get an older kid to buy it for them. They drink alone in their room and camouflage the evidence with breath mints, eyedrops, and lies.

Research shows that if you begin drinking at an early age, you are more likely to be a heavy drinker in your teen years and as an adult.

How your parents drink also influences your drinking habits. In fact, most kids get their first drink at home. Sipping from Dad's beer can or having a glass of sweet wine at a family celebration is the way most kids start. But alcoholism, the disease of drinking too much alcohol, develops more quickly and with less alcohol for teens than for adults. You can become an alcoholic in one or two years.

That doesn't mean you drink every day. But if you use alcohol on a regular basis and find that you can't stop, you have a problem. Beer and wine are just as addictive as the "hard" liquors such as scotch, vodka, and bourbon.

Many teens, and adults too, believe that beer and wine contain less alcohol than hard liquor. True beer (4 to 5 percent), wine (12 to 14 percent), and hard liquor (35 to 50 percent) do vary in content; it's how you drink them that equals it out. One 12-ounce can of beer, a five-ounce glass of wine, and a regular gin and tonic or vodka and orange juice all contain the same amount of alcohol. Without realizing it, you could be considered a problem drinker just by downing a few beers a day.

Weekly Reader, a magazine for elementary school children, obtained some startling results in a recent survey. Fourth-graders who were polled accepted wine coolers as "healthy fruit drinks." According to this drug-use survey, only 21 percent of these kids thought of wine coolers as a drug. More than 74 percent saw no harm in having one wine cooler daily! Wine cooler advertising is pretty successful, isn't it?

In reality, these "harmless" coolers contain approximately 5.5 percent alcohol, as much as beer. The fruity taste is very appealing to kids who are beginning to experiment with alcohol. *LISTEN*, a drug prevention magazine, calls wine coolers the "gateway drink" because the sweet taste and attractive packaging make them acceptable to people who are not used to drinking.

Most teens expect to have a great time when they drink.

"I can get silly and flirt with the older guys after two beers," Samantha said. "I think it makes me more attractive to them."

Samantha doesn't realize that the message she sends when she drinks is quite different from when she is sober. Are the boys more attracted to Sammi when she's "silly"? Or do they figure she's easy and looking for a "good time"?

The teen years are a time for separating from your parents and establishing your own identity. Teens want to be grown-up. Drinking is seen as an adult thing to do. Kids follow the role models set by their parents and by older teens. Your friends may push you to drink with them. Being an adult means making mature decisions. But teens who have been doing heavy-duty drinking for a few years are not always capable of making mature decisions. Their emotional development is stunted by alcohol.

Driving is one of the bridges you cross as you move toward adulthood. Getting your license means freedom, independence, and a huge step toward taking control of your own life.

Alcohol can give you a false sense of control. It slows down your reaction time in critical situations that can arise when you are driving. You love that sense of "hanging loose" and driving fast as the radio blasts in your car. Combine that scenario with a few drinks, and what you are driving turns into a lethal weapon. Thousands and thousands of teenagers are killed, maimed, or seriously injured in alcohol-related accidents each year.

What's the answer? What's my part in this? I'm only one kid, you say, I can't make any difference.

Yes, you can. If once, just once, you stop someone from driving drunk, you will very likely have saved his life or the lives of others. If you call your parents for a ride home instead of driving drunk, you may well have saved your own life. You can make a difference if you learn the skills necessary for *coping with drinking and driving*.

CHAPTER ◇ 3

What Alcohol Does to Your Body

Many teens do not consider alcohol a drug.

"My father has a couple of beers every night after work. And my grandmother drinks wine with every meal. That's what goes on in my house."

You probably live in a family where adults drink. Maybe you sipped a swig from your dad's beer as you were growing up. Perhaps you were allowed a glass of champagne on family holidays. Alcohol has been perceived throughout history as socially acceptable. Celebrating happy times and religious events keeps the refrigerator stocked or gives cause for a quick trip to the liquor store for many families.

But when alcohol is not used responsibly (that's the key word), it has the potential of becoming the main ingredient in a destructive death force.

SOME ALCOHOL FACTS

- Alcohol affects your entire body, with the most dangerous effects concentrating on your central nervous system, particularly your brain.
- In small doses, alcohol can be a stimulant (give you a feeling of being happy, silly, energetic). When taken in large doses, it is a brain depressant.
- How drunk you get depends on how fast you drink.
- Alcohol enters your bloodstream directly without being digested. Researchers say that small amounts are absorbed directly through the lining of your mouth and throat, going straight to your brain. It goes through the walls of your stomach and small intestine and is absorbed into your blood. From there it travels directly to your brain.
- Your body burns off the alcohol you drink at a constant rate. That rate is about one ounce of 100-proof liquor an hour. But if you drink more than you can eliminate, the drug accumulates in your body. You become intoxicated, which means that the *poisonous* or *toxic* effects of alcohol go into action in your brain and in your body.

FIVE STAGES OF INTOXICATION

This research is based on a 150-pound person. If you weigh less than that, the amount it takes to get drunk is less.

One drink is defined as: 5 ounces of wine, 12 ounces of beer, or 1½ ounces of hard liquor mixed in a drink.

Blood alcohol content (BAC) is a term that is used frequently in this book. Dr. Gail Milgram, Director of Edu-

Alcohol's In/Out Route

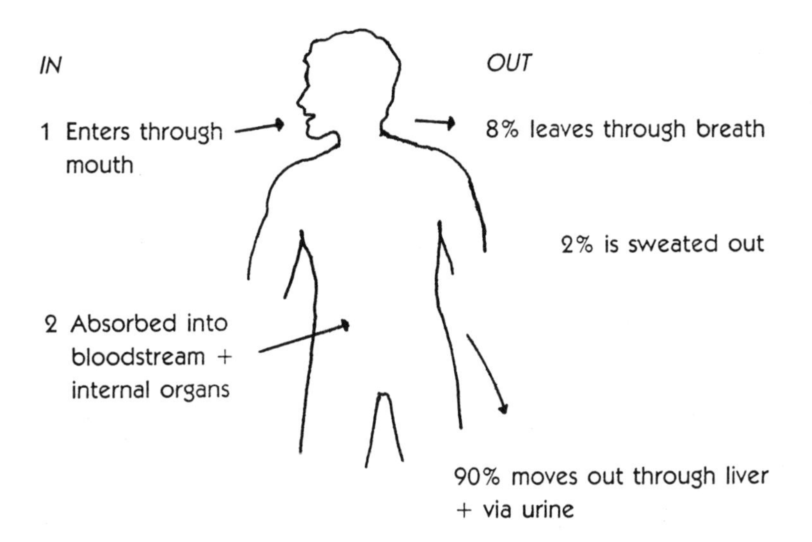

When you drink more than you eliminate, your brain function is affected.

12 Oz. Can Beer

5 Oz. Glass Wine

1 1/2 Oz. Distilled Beverages

cation and Training at the Center for Alcohol Studies, Rutgers University, defines BAC as "the term used to designate the amount of alcohol in a person's blood. The BAC is always written as a decimal part of 1%." A BAC of .1 means that you have one part alcohol to 1000 parts of blood in your body.

According to Dr. Milgram, "If a person's BAC were between 0.5 and 1 percent, the breathing center of the brain would be paralyzed and death would occur."

Stage 1. Two drinks within a two-hour time period. Your blood alcohol content reaches .05%, which means one part of alcohol to 2000 parts of your blood. You may feel happy, relaxed, talkative, flirty, and attractive to others.

Stage 2. Another drink or two will boost your BAC to .10% (one part alcohol to 1000 parts of blood). Alcohol becomes a depressant drug at this point and begins to interfere with brain activity. Your thoughts become muddled, your speech is a bit slurred.

Stage 3. Having four or five drinks within two hours boosts your BAC to .20%, which impairs your brain considerably. Staggering, loss of movement, sluggishness will severely limit your physical ability. Moodiness and depression can occur. (The angry drunk is a familiar person.) At this stage you need six to eight hours to return to normal.

Stage 4. With a .30 BAC (one part alcohol to 300 parts blood) you are in a drunken stupor. Six or seven drinks within two to four hours brings you to this stage. You are really out of it. You don't know what you are doing.

Stage 5. With a .40 or .50 BAC (one part alcohol to 250 or 200 parts blood), you are unconcious, blacked-out, or in a coma. The part of your brain that controls your breathing and heartbeat is severely affected. You could die because your respiratory system is paralyzed and you stop breathing.

The following information and charts give a more visual focus on the BAC picture. Dr. Marshall Stearn, in his book, *Drinking and Driving—Know Your Limits and Liabilities*, provided the information in conjunction with Allstate Insurance Company and the California Highway Patrol.

IT TAKES A LOT OF DRINK TO MAKE A DRUNK!

The examples that follow show the approximate *average* standard servings of liquor, beer, or wine that a 150-pound person would have to consume in a one-hour period to reach 0.10%, the percentage-weight of alcohol in the bloodstream (blood alcohol content or BAC) that is the threshold of driver intoxication in most states.

Equivalent standard servings for "one drink" are: 1¼ ounces of 80-proof liquor, 4 ounces of normal-strength table wine, and 12 ounces of normal-strength beer.

To determine the approximate average number of standard drinks needed in a one-hour period to reach 0.10%, draw a line from Body Weight to 0.10%. The line will intersect the average number of ounces needed to produce 0.10%. Follow the same procedure to determine the amount of liquor needed to reach other BACs, such as 0.05%, 0.15%, etc.

Charts show *rough averages only*. Many factors affect the rate of alcohol absorption into the bloodstream. Amount of food consumed, kind of food and drink consumed, and percentage of fatty tissue in the body, for examples, can vary BAC values.

The rate of elimination of alcohol from the bloodstream is approximately 0.015% per hour. Therefore, subtract

ESTIMATED AMOUNT OF 80 PROOF LIQUOR NEEDED TO REACH APPROXIMATE GIVEN LEVELS OF ALCOHOL IN THE BLOOD

"EMPTY STOMACH"

DURING A ONE-HOUR PERIOD*
WITH LITTLE OR NO FOOD INTAKE PRIOR TO DRINKING

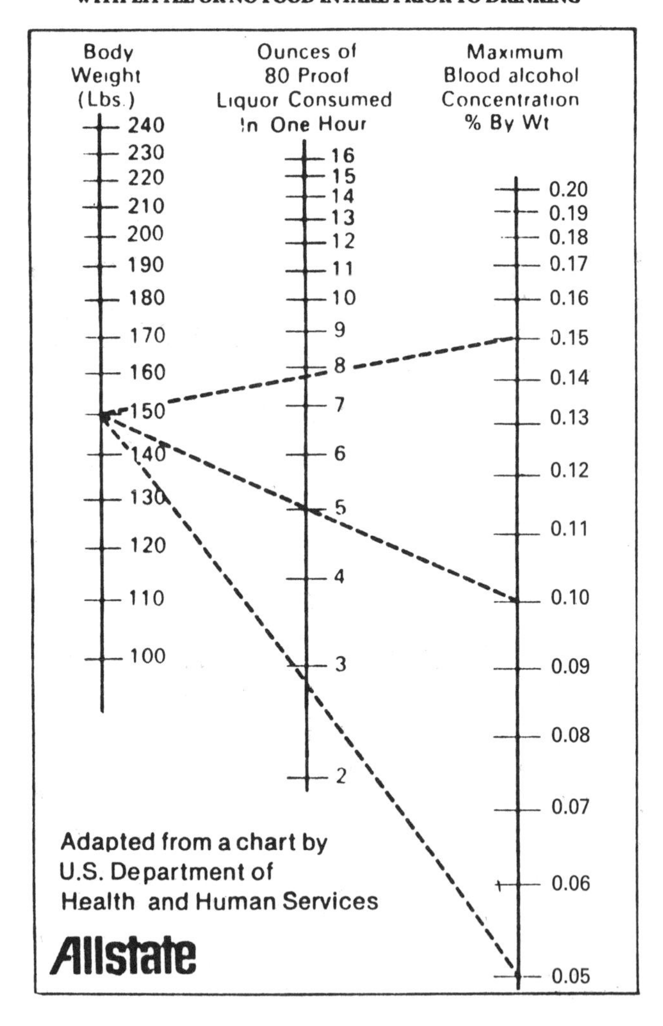

"FULL STOMACH"

DURING A ONE-HOUR PERIOD* OCCURRING BETWEEN ONE AND TWO HOURS AFTER AN AVERAGE MEAL

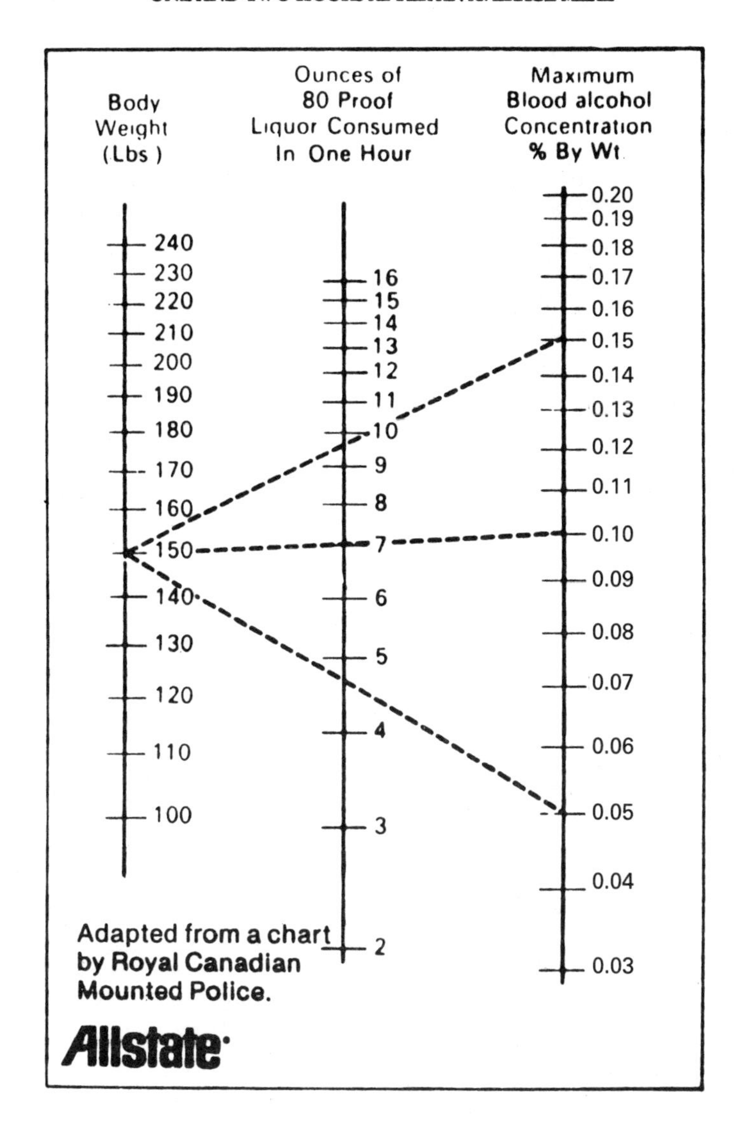

BAC Zones: 90 to 109 lbs.

TIME FROM 1st DRINK | TOTAL DRINKS 1 2 3 4 5 6 7 8

1 hr

2 hrs

3 hrs

4 hrs

(.01% – .04%) Seldom illegal

(.05% – .09%) May be illegal

(.10% Up) Definitely illegal

BAC Zones: 110 to 129 lbs.

TIME FROM 1st DRINK | TOTAL DRINKS 1 2 3 4 5 6 7 8

1 hr

2 hrs

3 hrs

4 hrs

(.01% – .04%) Seldom illegal

(.05% – .09%) May be illegal

(.10% Up) Definitely illegal

BAC Zones: 130 to 149 lbs.

TIME FROM 1st DRINK | TOTAL DRINKS 1 2 3 4 5 6 7 8

1 hr

2 hrs

3 hrs

4 hrs

(.01% – .04%) Seldom illegal

(.05% – .09%) May be illegal

(.10% Up) Definitely illegal

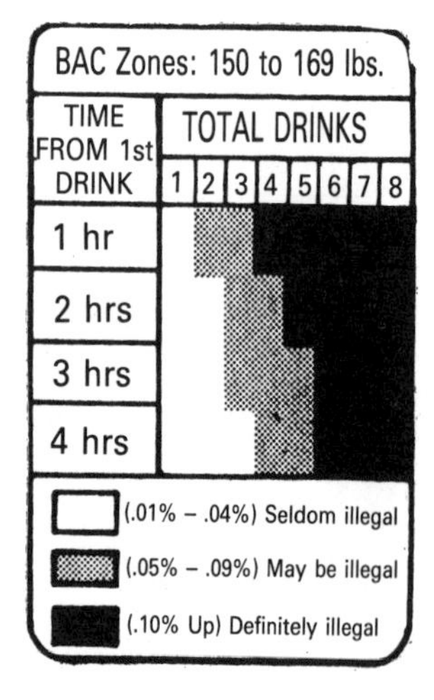

BAC Zones: 170 to 189 lbs.

TIME FROM 1st DRINK	TOTAL DRINKS							
	1	2	3	4	5	6	7	8
1 hr								
2 hrs								
3 hrs								
4 hrs								

(.01% – .04%) Seldom illegal
(.05% – .09%) May be illegal
(.10% Up) Definitely illegal

BAC Zones: 190 to 209 lbs.

TIME FROM 1st DRINK	TOTAL DRINKS							
	1	2	3	4	5	6	7	8
1 hr								
2 hrs								
3 hrs								
4 hrs								

(.01% – .04%) Seldom illegal
(.05% – .09%) May be illegal
(.10% Up) Definitely illegal

BAC Zones: 210 to 229 lbs.

TIME FROM 1st DRINK	TOTAL DRINKS							
	1	2	3	4	5	6	7	8
1 hr								
2 hrs								
3 hrs								
4 hrs								

(.01% – .04%) Seldom illegal
(.05% – .09%) May be illegal
(.10% Up) Definitely illegal

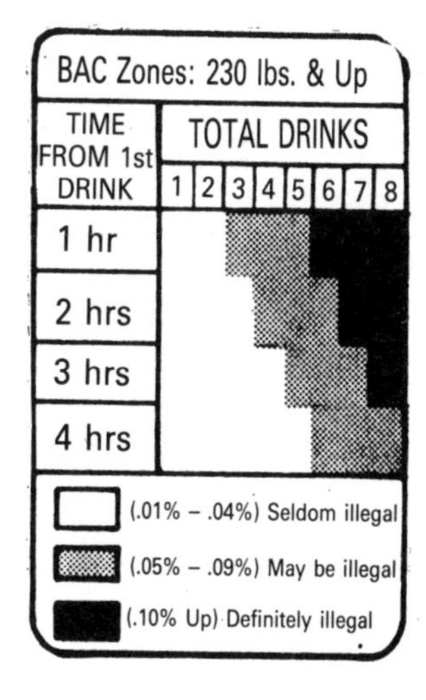

BREATH ALCOHOL CC

APPROXIMATE BREATH ALCOHOL CONCENTRATION (In Grams *)

Drinks ** In Body	Body Weight in Pounds							
	100	120	140	160	180	200	220	240
1	.04	.03	.03	.03	.02	.02	.02	.02
2	.08	.06	.05	.05	.04	.04	.03	.03
3	.11	.09	.08	.07	.06	.06	.05	.05
4	.15	.12	.11	.09	.08	.08	.07	.06
5	.19	.16	.13	.12	.11	.09	.09	.08
6	.23	.19	.16	.14	.13	.11	.10	.09
7	.26	.22	.19	.16	.15	.13	.12	.11
8	.30	.25	.21	.19	.17	.15	.14	.13
9	.34	.28	.24	.21	.19	.17	.15	.14
10	.38	.31	.27	.23	.21	.19	.17	.16
11		.40	.34	.30	.27	.24	.22	.20
12			.38	.33	.29	.26	.24	.22
13			.40	.36	.32	.29	.26	.24
14				.38	.34	.31	.28	.26
15					.37	.33	.30	.28

*Alcohol concentration is expressed here as grams of alcohol per 210 liters of brea 10 one-hundredths (10/100) grams of alcohol per 210 liters of breath.

**A drink is defined as: 1½ oz. of 80 proof liquor or 12 oz. of beer or 5 oz. of table wine hour of drinking after the first hour.

 ***National Safety Council***

ENT AND ITS EFFECTS

:ffects on Feeling and 3ehavior	Effects on Driving Ability
ᐱbsence of observable effects. Mild alteration of 'eelings, slight intensifica- tion of existing moods.	Mild changes. Most driv- ers seem a bit moody. Bad driving habits slightly pronounced.
'eeling of relaxation. Mild edation. Exaggeration of emotions and behavior. ;light impairment of motor ;kills. Increase in reaction 'ime.	Drivers take too long to decide and act. Motor skills (such as braking) are impaired. Reaction time is increased.
)ifficulty performing gross notor skills. Uncoordinated behavior. Definite impair- nent of mental abilities, udgment, and memory.	Judgment seriously af- fected. Physical and mental coordination im- paired. Physical difficulty in driving a vehicle.
Major impairment of all physical and mental unctions. Irresponsible behavior. Euphoria. Some difficulty standing, walk- ng, and talking.	Distortion of all percep- tion and judgment. Driv- ing erratic. Driver in a daze.
ᐱt .40, most people have passed out. Hospitalization is probable at BACs of .40 and above, and death is mminent.	It is hoped that the driver passed out before trying to get into vehicle.

} of ".10" on a breath-testing instrument indicates

ɿe drink, from the number consumed, for each

0.015% from blood alcohol content indicated on the charts for each hour after the start of drinking.

There is no safe way to drive after drinking. These charts show that a few drinks can make you an unsafe driver. They show that drinking affects your blood alcohol content (BAC). The BAC zones for various numbers of drinks and time periods are printed in white, gray, and black.

How to use these charts on pages 24–25: First, find the chart that includes your weight. For example, if you weigh 160 lbs., use the "150 to 169" chart. Then look under "Total Drinks" at the "2" on this "150 to 169" chart. Now look below the "2" drinks, in the row for 1 hour. You'll see your BAC is in the gray shaded zone. This means that if you drive after 2 drinks in 1 hour, you could be arrested. In the gray zone, your chances of having an accident are 5 times higher than if you had no drinks. But, if you had 4 drinks in 1 hour, your BAC would be in the black shaded area...and your chances of having an accident 25 times higher. What's more, it is *illegal* to drive at this BAC (.10% or greater). Before reaching the white BAC zone again, the chart shows you would need 4 hours...with no more drinks.

As you begin to drink and continue to drink, you can develop a tolerance. That means that your brain can change its sensitivity to alcohol and "tolerate" higher levels. This can lead to addiction and dependence. The disease of alcoholism becomes your way of life.

The above stages vary with your weight. A girl of 110 pounds needs less than her boyfriend of 170 pounds to reach the higher stages of intoxication.

How fast you drink also affects your BAC. If you chug

a few beers one right after another, you will be affected much more than your friend who sips the same amount.

Drinking on an empty stomach speeds alcohol's effects. It is absorbed faster and hits you harder than drinking with a full stomach.

Your mood at the time you drink, the tolerance you've built up to alcohol, your experience with drinking, and your tiredness or fatigue are also contributing factors to how drunk you can get and how fast it happens.

The only thing that can sober you up is *time*. Your body needs hours to eliminate the liquor you've drunk. Nothing can speed up that process. Drinking tons of coffee will only make you a wide-awake drunk, not sober. Cold showers will make you a shivering, wet drunk. Only giving your liver time to metabolize and get rid of the alcohol is the real key to sobering up.

CHAPTER ◇ 4

Why Do Teens Drink?

"To have fun."

"I feel more happy and attractive. My boyfriend likes it when I loosen up."

"It's easier to get along at parties when I have a few beers. I'm not so shy anymore."

"It gets me going so I can dance and have a good time."

It seems that everyone has a favorite funny drinking story. Remember when Micah Jones tossed all the empty beer cans in the town fountain and then jumped in himself?

Or when Sheila Masi polished off that pint of gin and slept it off on the football bleachers all night? Har har. Way to go, Sheila.

Remember prom night when Tommy Thompson barfed purple all over his white tux from those sloe gin fizzes he had? Outasite, Tommy!

Who has the funniest story? Who laughs the loudest at these hilarious escapades?

Do you think it was Tommy's date who got splashed with Tommy's purple barf all over her $200 prom dress?

Or maybe it was Sheila's parents who reported her missing to the police and stayed up all night driving around town looking for her?

Or do you think that the young pregnant woman who was going to pick up her husband at work when Micah ran her off the road after he sloshed out of the fountain had a good laugh?

Sobering thoughts? Not to Micah, Sheila, or Tommy, who followed up these episodes with even more outrageously "funny" behavior. These kids forgot that there are consequences involved with drinking. What you do affects other people.

Television and print ads try to convince you that it's cool and grown-up to drink. Being sociable and accepted by a group of friends is important to teenagers. Kids drink for other reasons too:

- Tension or anxiety ("I had a tough day. I need a drink.")
- Alienation and loneliness ("There's nobody to hang out with. Who wants a loser like me?")
- Boredom ("What else is there to do around here anyway?")
- Disappointment and bitterness ("There's Carrie with her new boyfriend. She'll probably give him the ax like she did me.")
- Sadness ("Life sucks.")
- Anger ("I am so sick of my parents criticizing everything I do. Get me another can of beer, will ya?")
- Enjoyment ("I like to drink. It's fun.")
- Experimentation ("It's just something I'm trying out. I can handle it.")
- Emotional turmoil ("Look, my parents just went

through the worst divorce. Drinking helps blot out my reality right now.")
- Peer pressure ("I'm no baby. I can drink you under the table, big shot. Watch me.")

"You want to know the real reason I drink at parties?" Sasha, a sophomore, asked. "I feel sexy and the boys like me a lot when I'm high, so I'm popular at parties. I always get to go home with somebody in his car. We park for a while and have a good time. It gets me some love."

For Sasha, losing her inhibitions is important. How else could she give herself permission to experiment with sex? Aren't teens supposed to try things out? Isn't it cool to get picked up at a party by someone you don't know and then get hot and heavy with him in the back seat of his car? Doesn't it make you popular? What does Sasha think of herself the next morning? And why does she do this again and again?

Looking for love stems from feeling unloved either at home or by the opposite sex. Drinking sometimes helps you to lose your inhibitions, but as you continue to drink, the decision-making part of your brain gets muddled, and you may make the wrong decision or no decision at all. Serious consequences can follow that route of action.

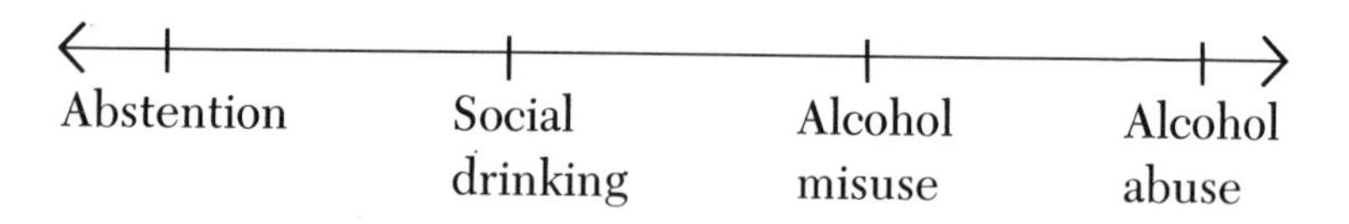

Along the continuum of drinking, teens need to assess their position. Between abstention and social drinking certainly is the safest life area in which to be. Social drinking involves slow, recreational consumption as part of a family gathering or special event. Negative consequences are few when one has one glass of wine at a cousin's bar mitzvah.

Alcohol misuse moves you into an area where there are obvious negative consequences. Acting inappropriately or aggressively are symptoms of misuse. Misuse is usually infrequent.

Alcohol abuse, at the extreme end of the continuum, is like misuse except that it occurs on a regular basis.

Your place on the continuum may vary. But as you move further to the right, you severely jeopardize your safety and the safety of others.

Moving from childhood to adulthood is an enormous transition. You seek independence and grown-up status. You want control of your own life, and you need to experiment with new behaviors to see if they fit the emerging adult "you." Imitating the "adult" behaviors of drinking may seem important at this time.

CHAPTER ◇ 5

High School Habits

In 1988 the Institute for Social Research at the University of Michigan, Ann Arbor, conducted a cumulative survey called "Drinking and Driving Among American High School Seniors."

The statistics for the survey were compiled by Patrick O'Malley, PhD, and Lloyd Johnston, PhD, for their project, Monitoring the Future. Across the nation more than 17,000 high school seniors were polled about their driving, drinking, and drinking/driving habits. The information in the accompanying chart was presented as testimony at hearings held by the National Commission against Drunk Driving and the National Highway Traffic Safety Administration on March 29, 1988.

When asked how many had used alcohol in the previous thirty days, the seniors surveyed reported a 69.7 percent use in 1982. The percentage declined to 65.3 percent in 1986 and rose slightly to 66.4 percent in 1987.

"Kids are drinking, no doubt about that," said seventeen-year-old Linda. "Hanging out on weekends with not much to do brings on the party scene. In my crowd, I'd say that 80 to 90 percent drink a couple weekends a month."

1988 Survey

Drinking and Driving Among American High School Seniors

Institute for Social Research
The University of Michigan
Ann Arbor, Michigan

	1982	1983	1984	1985	1986	1987
Percent Having Used Alcohol in Past 30 Days:	69.7	69.4	67.2	65.9	65.3	66.4
Percent Drinking Five or More Drinks in a Row in Past Two Weeks:	40.5	40.8	38.7	36.7	36.8	37.5
Percent Driving After Drinking Alcohol:	—	—	31.2	29.0	26.8	26.6
Percent Driving After Having Five or More Drinks:	—	—	18.3	16.6	15.8	15.0
Percent Riding as Passenger After Driver Had Been Drinking Alcohol:	—	—	44.2	39.1	38.2	38.2
Percent Riding as Passenger After Driver Had Five or More Drinks:	—	25.4	21.5	21.2	21.9	—
Percent of Seniors Using Seatbelts When Driving:						
Never, Seldom	—	—	—	—	43.2	36.7
Always	—	—	—	—	25.0	33.0
Percent Reporting One or More Accidents in Past 12 Months:	22.2	22.2	22.8	24.4	25.1	25.6
Percent Having One or More Accidents After Alcohol Use in Past 12 Months:	3.3	3.0	2.8	2.7	2.2	2.5
Percent Reporting One or More Moving Violations in Past 12 Months:	24.8	27.1	26.5	27.6	30.4	31.7
Percent Cited for Moving Violation After Alcohol Use in Past 12 Months:	5.0	5.1	4.5	4.4	4.3	4.6

Depending on your group of friends, your crowd may drink very little or they may push drinking as a requirement to stay in with the crowd. The decisions you make about how much and when you drink can affect many aspects of your life—peer group acceptance, problems with your parents, sexual complications, academics, problems with the police, and so on.

The 66.4 percent may include kids who perhaps had one or two beers in the previous few weeks. However, the next group of seniors, who had five or more drinks in a row (on one occasion) in the past two weeks, showed a slight decline from 40.5 percent in 1982 to 37.5 percent in 1987. As was shown in the BAC charts in Chapter 3, five drinks in a row without many hours elapsing between them can give you a BAC of almost .2 if you weigh 100 lbs., .12 if you weigh 160 lbs., and .09 (almost .10) if you weigh 200 to 220 lbs. That many drinks puts you in the legally drunk and judgmentally inpaired status. And that's almost 38 percent, or more than one third, of the seniors surveyed. Getting drunk and being legally unsafe to drive one or more times every two weeks seems to be the recreation of choice for one out of three high school seniors.

In 1987 seniors who drove after drinking alcohol registered at 26.6 percent. That's more than one fourth of the kids surveyed. Some of them may have had only one drink and would not be considered legally drunk. But even a small amount of alcohol can impair your coordination, judgment, and brain activity depending on how much food you've eaten, what your frame of mind is, and how much you weigh.

In 1984, 18.3 percent admitted to driving after having five or more drinks in a row. That statistic dropped to 15 percent in 1987, but a serious problem still exists.

"More of my friends are staying over at the house where

the party is," said Kevin, sixteen. "That way they don't have to worry about driving or getting into an accident. It saves on hassles from parents too. But it does make the party last longer; kids don't plan on going home, so they drink more."

"I had a party and my parents took everyone's keys away," said Krisann, seventeen. "They were pretty nervous about anyone driving. My father was in an accident with a drunk driver years ago, so we've always been careful about it. The kids had to get the keys back from Mom or Dad if they wanted to drive home."

Kids trust their lives to others who've been drinking more than they trust themselves to drive after drinking. In the survey, the percentage of seniors who rode as a passenger with a driver who had been drinking topped 40 percent over the course of the survey. That's almost one out of two teenagers.

Seniors who rode with a legally drunk driver (one who had had five or more drinks in a row) declined from 25.4 to

PASSENGER VEHICLE DEATHS BY AGE, SEX, AND SEATING POSITION, 1987

	Drivers		Passengers	
Age	Male	Female	Male	Female
13	4	2	59	41
14	21	11	91	85
15	64	26	163	144
16	335	191	261	180
17	450	216	312	201
18	619	224	299	166
19	624	206	301	147

TEENAGE MOTOR VEHICLE DEATHS BY VEHICLE TYPE, 1987

Age	Pass. Vehicles	Motor-cycles	Pedes-trians	Bicycles	Other*
13	115	13	54	51	14
14	224	36	49	41	8
15	426	74	73	53	23
16	1,003	83	67	30	16
17	1,210	148	83	24	12
18	1,353	186	94	26	24
19	1,314	215	106	24	25

* includes unknowns

DISTRIBUTION (PERCENT) OF TEENAGE MOTOR VEHICLE FATALITIES BY TYPE OF VEHICLE, 1987

Age	Pass. Vehicles	Motor-cycles	Pedes-trians	Bicycles	Other
13	47	5	22	21	5
14	63	10	14	12	1
15	67	12	11	8	2
16	84	7	6	3	1
17	82	10	6	2	0
18	81	11	6	2	1
19	78	13	6	1	1

21.9 percent, but that means that one fourth of you will still get into a car with a driver who should not be on the road.

Look at the accompanying charts provided by the Insurance Institute for Highway Safety (IIHS).

Being both drivers and passengers, teenagers are involved in motor vehicle accidents in a disproportionate ratio to people of other ages. That means that the highest percentage of victims of car crashes are kids of high school age. In 1987 almost 7,300 teens ages thirteen to nineteen died in motor vehicle accidents. Almost 3,000 of them were not driving; they were trusting passengers.

From ages thirteen to fifteen to the sixteen to nineteen age group, there is a dramatic increase in deaths from car crashes per 100,000 people. For teenage boys the risks are greater; twice as many are killed as teenage girls. Males especially in the eighteen to nineteen-year-old group involve more deaths than any other group (34 per 100,000 people). That figure is double the death rate for thirty- to fifty-four-year-old males, an age group that spans twenty-four years.

Also in 1987, according to *IIHS Facts '88*, kids who were passengers died at a male/female ratio less than that of driver deaths. That means that of the passengers killed who were male, 12 per 100,000 were recorded versus 8 per 100,000 for females. The driver deaths were 17 per 100,000 males versus 7 per 100,000 females.

Does that mean that boyfriends are killing their girlfriends who happen to be passengers in their cars or light trucks at an alarming rate?

The statistics gathered by the IIHS do not reveal what part alcohol played in these car crashes and deaths, but you can compare the senior survey with the IIHS statistics and decide for yourself.

When do teens drink? When are the "best" parties? On the weekend, of course. According to IIHS, almost 60 percent of all teenage motor vehicle deaths happen on Friday, Saturday, or Sunday.

What time do you go out to drink? Nothing happens until late night, right? Look at this chart from IIHS.

PERCENT OF TEENAGE DEATHS OCCURRING AT NIGHT (9PM–6AM)

Age	Male	Female
13–15	31	39
16–17	48	44
18–19	59	48

About half of all kids killed in cars die between 9 pm and 6 am. When you get into a car with friends or if you yourself drive on a weekend, late at night, think about those statistics.

DRIVER DEATHS PER 100,000 PEOPLE, 1987

Age	Male	Female
0–12	—	—
13	—	—
14	1	1
15	4	2
16	17	10
17	23	12
18	34	13
19	34	11
20–24	29	9
25–29	22	7
30–64	13	5
65–74	14	5
75+	23	5

PASSENGER DEATHS, PER 100,000 PEOPLE, 1987

Age	Male	Female
0–12	3	3
13	4	3
14	5	5
15	9	8
16	13	10
17	16	11
18	16	9
19	16	8
20–24	11	5
25–29	5	3
30–64	2	3
65–74	3	5
75+	5	7

Most teenage passenger deaths (more than 62 percent) occur in crashes when another teen is driving. Forty-two percent of the motor vehicle deaths of thirteen- to seventeen-year-old passengers in 1987 happened when they got in a car with a sixteen- to seventeen-year-old behind the wheel.

Per mile facts for 1987 show that teenagers are involved in double the number of alcohol-related fatal crashes as drivers in the thirty- to forty-four-year-old age group, which spans twenty-four years.

The senior survey found that between 1982 and 1987 seniors reporting one or more moving violations (speeding, running a stop sign or a red light, etc.) in a twelve-month period rose from 24.8 to 31.7 percent.

Almost 5 percent reported that they were cited for a moving violation after using alcohol in the same twelve-month period. Added together, that means that over thirty-six percent of those seniors were stopped and ticketed or arrested for violations or driving under the influence (DUI).

"There's a lot more going on than that, I think," said eighteen-year-old Jose. "I have friends who have been stopped a couple of times. The cop asked them if they had been drinking and they said no. Then the cop gave them a speeding ticket or just let them go without checking them for drinking. And they were pretty drunk."

So statistics may not always be 100 percent accurate, but if the above information is 80 or 90 percent right it is still too many kids killed. If you were to poll your friends in your own informal survey and look to your own behavior, you might come up with similiar statistics or perhaps some even more frightening. Kids do drink and drive, even if they do not admit it on a national survey.

CHAPTER ◇ 6

Alcoholic Impairment of Driving Skills

In his book *Drinking and Driving—Know Your Limits and Liabilities*, Dr. Marshall Stearn documents the following experiment.

The Madigan Army Hospital, Tacoma, Washington, demonstrated one Memorial Day weekend the effects of a high-speed car crash. For a safety campaign, they sent a mannequin in a car moving at fifty-five miles per hour crashing into a tree. With time-lapse photography, the following graphic sequence of events was shown:

1/10 of a second after impact:

The front bumper and chrome frosting of the grillwork collapse. Slivers of steel penetrate the tree to a depth of over one inch.

2/10 of a second after impact:

The hood crumples and smashes into the windshield. Spinning rear wheels leave the ground. As the fenders come into contact with the tree, the car bends in the middle, with the rear end buckling over the front end.

3/10 of a second after impact:

The mannequin's body is now off the seat, upright, knees pressing against the dashboard. The plastic and steel frame of the steering wheel begins to bend under the weight of the mannequin. Its head is near the sun visor, the chest above the steering column.

4/10 of a second after impact:

The car's front twenty-four inches have been demolished, but the rear end is still traveling at an estimated thirty-five miles per hour. The mannequin is still traveling at fifty-five miles per hour. The half-ton engine block crunches into the tree. The rear end of the car, still bucking like a horse, rises high enough to scrape bark off low branches.

5/10 of a second after impact:

The mannequin's hands, frozen onto the steering wheel, bend the steering column into an almost vertical position. The force of gravity then pushes it into the steering column.

6/10 of a second after impact:

The brake pedal shears off at the floorboard. The chassis bends in the middle, shearing body bolts. The rear of the car begins to fall back down; its spinning wheels dig into the ground.

7/10 of a second after impact:

The seat of the car rams forward, pinning the mannequin against the steering shaft; the hinges tear, and the doors spring open.

* * *

Close your eyes and see yourself as the driver of that car or the passenger. It doesn't take much imagination to conjure up the ghastly picture of what happens. Even if you were the best driver in the world, it would be almost impossible to respond quickly enough to such an emergency. Seven tenths of a second and it's over.

Add to that scenario the effect of alcohol on the driver. Making immediate and appropriate judgments in trying to avoid this tragic event is not possible. Alcohol impairs every skill you need to drive safely.

ALCOHOL AFFECTS VISION

Since alcohol is a depressant, it relaxes all the muscles of your body. You have less control over your muscles, including those that move and focus your eyes.

When the eye is working soberly, light enters through the pupil and goes through the lens. That focuses light rays on the retina. If something interferes with this process, the impulses, or messages, that are sent to the brain are incorrect or distorted. If a fuzzy picture is sent to the brain, your mind cannot correctly interpret the traffic scene in front of you.

ALCOHOL AFFECTS EYE FOCUS

A muscle in your eye automatically brings into focus objects both near and far. With the muscle-relaxing effect of alcohol, that muscle cannot function properly, and you don't see clearly. Your ability to focus is hampered, and what is in front of you is blurry.

ALCOHOL AFFECTS HOW MUCH LIGHT ENTERS YOUR EYES

The pupil of your eye acts like the shutter of a camera to let in just the right amount of light. The pupil narrows when bright light shines in your eye, to avoid damage to the retina. In the dark, the pupil opens to admit more light so that you can see better.

Did you ever shine a flashlight in your eyes? It takes about one second for the pupils to constrict to keep all that light out. Then when you turn the flashlight off, everything seems black and blurry until your pupils open again to admit light. When you are driving at night and the headlight glare of oncoming cars hits your eyes, the same thing happens. It takes one second for your pupils to constrict and seven seconds to adapt again to the dark.

When you are drinking it doesn't happen that fast. Your pupils constrict, but it takes longer to recover. So you wind up driving semiblind for several seconds.

ALCOHOL PRODUCES DOUBLE VISION

Six muscles act to make your eyes work together. When those six muscles are impaired by alcohol, focusing on the same point by both your eyes is affected. Double vision results. Your brain has to interpret *two* messages it is receiving from your eyes. Your brain may read that two cars are approaching you, with four headlights glaring into your eyes. Which of the two cars do you react to? Which headlights do you veer away from?

Also, when your brain receives double messages it picks up on the stronger image. It's like driving with one eye closed: You have difficulty deciding exactly how far away that car is. Your depth perception is incorrect.

ALCOHOL AFFECTS YOUR DISTANCE JUDGMENT

Judging distance is one of the hardest things to learn when you start to drive. When you practiced parallel parking, did you set up orange cones or garbage cans to represent other cars and then spend hours knocking them down? Weren't you glad that all those dents were in the garbage cans and not in another car?

Your eyes need to work together to judge distances. Changing lanes, passing another car, and all the other things you do as you drive depend on how well you can judge distances. Your two eyes send two pictures to your brain, and you want those pictures to be coordinated exactly and synthesized so that you can correctly calculate the distance needed to change lanes or to park.

When you are drinking, your eyes don't work together, and no clearly coordinated picture is sent to your brain. Did you ever see a movie where the drunk keeps blinking his eyes because he is seeing double? We laugh as the camera shows us how funny it is for this guy who can't see straight. It gets unfunny pretty fast when that kind of guy gets in a car and is driving straight at you.

ALCOHOL AFFECTS PERIPHERAL VISION

When you are driving you see what's ahead of you on the road. You also notice things such as street signs, billboards, buildings, houses, and other cars. Even though you may not see these objects at the side clearly, you are aware that they are there. That is peripheral vision.

Being able to see cars coming out of intersections or driveways, or reacting when people walk out into the road or between cars is a crucial ability when driving. One study of peripheral vision and drinking indicated that a person with a blood alcohol content (BAC) of .055 (that's only one or two drinks in two hours for some people) lost 30 percent on a field of vision test. If you notice fewer dangers on either side of you as you drive, you increase your chances of having an accident.

Your speed also affects your peripheral vision. At 30 miles per hour you reduce your side vision by 25 percent. That means you see only three fourths of the things on the side of you as you drive. At 45 mph you reduce your side vision by 50 percent. That means you see only half of the things on the side. Speeding over 60 mph, you really are driving with "tunnel vision"; you see very little of what's on the side. Add the effects of alcohol to the decrease in peripheral vision and you get one drunk driver who sees almost nothing outside of the blurry, distorted scene right in front of him.

ALCOHOL AFFECTS NIGHT VISION

Seeing in the dark is difficult. We are not cats, with a special ability to see clearly at night. The rods and cones that make up the retina in the back of the eyeball are connected by nerves, which send pictures of what you see to the brain. The retina is like the film in a camera. The cones send the color images, and the rods transmit light and dark. The center of the retina has a density of cones, and that is where details such as traffic signs can be seen.

Alcohol reduces the oxygen in the bloodstream, which in turn affects the cones in the retina. The sharpness of the image you have when sober is reduced, and it becomes blurry. This visual acuity or sharpness is already reduced by over one half at night when you are sober. When you drink and drive, it is greatly reduced.

Research done on dark adaptation (seeing clearly at low light levels) indicates that the ability to detect low-contrast, low-illumination targets is impaired when the BAC is .08 percent or higher. That is still under the .10 percent for you to be considered legally drunk.

ALCOHOL AFFECTS DRIVING TIME-SHARING SKILLS

When you drive, you have to monitor many things at once. Your attention is divided among the many tasks and skills needed to drive safely. The computer in your brain receives input from what you see and do as you drive.

A beginning driver does not have the years of practice to be able to coordinate and mentally process all the information you gather as you drive. In addition to all the things you need to watch for and the skills you need to drive safely, add effects of alcohol, loud radio, and distractions from your passengers. All this incoming data must be analyzed by your brain. Then you make and execute decisions based on your conclusions.

Recently in New Jersey, a group of students decided to spend the day at a nearby amusement park. They crowded nine people into a car designed for five. As the driver tried to light a cigarette, she let a front-seat passenger hold the steering wheel. The car crashed, killing two of the teenagers and injuring the others.

By "sharing" her attention with the cigarette, she did not give full attention to driving.

ALCOHOL AFFECTS VISUAL SEARCH AND RECOGNITION SKILLS

Continual observation of all the things you see as you drive—such as other cars moving in your direction or oncoming, stop lights, traffic signs to stop, yield, or give right-of-way, parked cars, pedestrians, motorcycles, bicycles, and road conditions—is vital to safety. You must constantly be alert and on the lookout for things that can mean the difference between a safe ride home and an accident. You use your visual search and recognition skills to sort out all that you observe as you drive.

Just looking out the windshield won't take in all that requires your attention. Using the rearview mirror and the side mirrors, turning your head to see out the side windows or the back, and checking the blind spots of your car are all part of searching out and recognizing potential problems.

In laboratory tests and in a report by the U.S. Department of Transportation, it has been documented that drinking affects how you divide your attention among the tasks necessary to drive safely. Alcohol impairs the rate at which your brain can process information, thereby interfering with your ability to divide your attention among things your brain is telling you.

"Watch for that car coming up on your right," your brain tells you. "Get ready to make a right turn," is also in your mind. *LOOK OUT*! You forgot to check that blind spot at the back corner of the car and you ran a driver off the road when you turned right.

ALCOHOL AFFECTS TRACKING SKILLS

Did you ever watch a seven-year-old drive a steering wheel on one of those arcade video games? Little kids "drive" by yanking the wheel back and forth, to the left, to the right, again and again. If you were in a car with a driver like that, you'd probably feel seasick.

Tracking skills involve using the steering wheel. What

you see through the windshield is translated by your brain into correct movements of your hands on the steering wheel. To keep your car in the right lane of traffic, make a left turn, or negotiate a turn, you need sharp tracking skills and plenty of practice.

Backing up is difficult to learn because your brain needs to register tracking information while your body is turned around. It becomes confusing, and your attention needs to be sharp, especially on wet or icy nights.

"My boyfriend only had a few beers. I thought he was okay to drive," Maura said. "But when we hit that curve, we skidded over onto the shoulder and almost hit a tree. He says it was icy. I say he was going a little too fast. Maybe it was the beers too. Whatever the real reason, we were really shook up. I never told my parents, because we weren't hurt or crashed or anything like that. But I was afraid to drive with my boyfriend for a while after that night."

ALCOHOL AFFECTS YOUR REACTION TIME

Consider this. You're in your best friend's car. His older brother Jack is driving and seems to be a little high. He is cruising along, paying more attention to finding the hot radio station he likes than to driving. All of a sudden you see a van coming out of the intersection right in front of you. It's running the stop sign, and Jack is still fooling with the radio. You scream "*Stop!*" Will Jack react in time?

Reaction time, which is the time it takes to begin responding to a situation, is crucial in driving. Slamming on your brakes, veering to the side of the road, scooting into the other lane to avoid an accident require quick reactions in addition to all the above-mentioned driving skills.

Having to combine several skills with a quick reaction time, drivers with alcohol in their blood are not as effective in putting it all together. When you get in a car, your chances of being in an accident are one in seven. When you get in a car slightly drunk or with a drunk driver, your chances drop to one in three. Choose your odds.

Any drug is a mind-altering drug. Alcohol is a drug. It depresses the central nervous system. When you consume large quantities of alcohol, you can come to the point of falling into a stupor, getting "wasted," drinking to a "falling-down drunk" stage, passing out—whatever you want to call it. Doing that in a car could take a life—yours or someone else's.

When you drink small amounts, alcohol can initially make you feel stimulated. You feel flushed. Your heart beats faster. You speak quickly, and you may feel pretty good. You lose some of your inhibitions and feel freer to laugh, talk, dance, fool around. That carries over when you get behind the wheel of your car.

"When I'm drinking, I feel braver," Luke remarked. "My friends and I like to play 'chicken' when we drive—you know, when you keep passing each other? I'm not as scared if I'm a little drunk."

Fear reduction and risk-taking seem to come about as a result of drinking. Your emotional and psychological states undergo a change when you consume a mind-altering drug. Kids take risks that they never would take sober.

Aggressive tendencies may come to the surface. There's always one person in every crowd who fights when he or she gets drunk. Put that person behind the wheel and look out; he or she is the one who will tailgate or shine the high beams at you if he doesn't like the way you are driving.

* * *

"I'm okay to drive," is the oft-repeated statement when a party is breaking up. Believing that your driving skills are as good when you are drinking as when you are sober is also a common effect of alcohol. In one test study, drivers knocked over orange cones and ran down flags, but they still felt that they drove as well as they did when not drinking. Delusions of alcohol. To drive safely and minimize the risks of getting into an accident, you need to be sharp, alert, and in control. Drinking interferes with your emotions, your brain, your coordination, and all the skills necessary to drive safely.

CHAPTER ◇ 7

Familiar Scenarios

Drinking responsibly involves deliberate decision-making. Deciding on the safe, correct, responsible course of action on the spur of the moment or under pressure from your friends isn't easy. Weighing the consequences of your decisions takes time and thought. Some teenagers give in to impulsive decisions. That might be because you have never been in that particular situation before and have no experience or history on which to draw.

To give you some practice in drinking and driving decision-making, here are some scenarios in which you might become involved. They are followed by open-ended questions for you to test out your decision-making skills. There is no pat answer or single action that will work in every situation. Much is left up to you here as it will be in real life.

SCENARIO #1

Your drama club has worked for months on your production of *Grease*. Your final performance was exhilarating but also sad. The closeness your group had developed is at an end. Things will never be the same again. So you're happy and smiling, but feeling a little empty inside.

The cast party is at Marcy's house. When you walk in, platters of food are all over the kitchen table. As you load your plate, you see that the fridge is filled with beer and soda.

You overhear Marcy's mother telling another parent, "I know these kids will drink somewhere tonight, so it might as well be here. This way I can watch them."

— Do you agree with Marcy's mom? Why or why not?
— Was having a beer or another alcoholic drink the first thing on your mind after the final curtain went down?
— As you reach in the fridge what do you grab, the soda or the beer?
— Will the food and drinks quench your hunger and thirst or will you be looking to fill up that empty, sad feeling inside?
— Have a pretend discussion with your parents about this situation.
— Would your parents agree with Marcy's mother? Would they do the same thing at your house?
— It's the middle of the party. What kind of drink is in your hand now?
— How are you getting home? In whose car will you put your tired body and trust that you will be driven home safely?

SCENARIO #2

Your best friend got really drunk at a party. You feel a responsibility to take him home. As he lurches and trips up the steps to his front door, the porch light flashes on and there are his parents staring accusingly at you from behind the screen door.

— What do you say to his parents?
— How did you get him home? If you drove, were you in condition to do that and take risks?
— Was it really your responsibility to get your friend home, or could you have walked away and just taken care of yourself?
— What would you do if his parents blamed you for the condition he's in and threatened to call your parents?
— Have a pretend discussion with your parents about this situation. What would you say? How would they react? In real life would you be able to have that kind of discussion with them?
— What would you say to your friend the next day?
— What would you say to his parents the next day?

SCENARIO #3

You and your boyfriend/girlfriend just had the biggest fight in a long series of arguments. You are on the verge of breaking up, and you're feeling really mixed up about it. You are at a blast of a graduation party, and you want to have a good time even though he/she is there too.

— How are you feeling in your heart? How will that affect your decision whether to drink or how much to drink?
— You drove your father's new sports car tonight because yours had a flat tire—and you wanted to show off a little to make you feel better. How

will that influence your decision about drinking tonight?

— Someone shoves a rum and Coke in your hand, light on the Coke and heavy on the rum. What do you do?

— An old crush whom you'd like to impress comes along and dances real close with you for a few slow dances. Then he/she mentions that a different kind of "party" is going on upstairs. "Come on up" is the invitation. You know that dope and sex are going on. You're feeling lonely and would like to be with someone tonight. What do you do?

— Later you see your almost-ex boyfriend/girlfriend sitting alone and pretty much wasted. Would you go over? What would you say? Could you walk away and say it's not your problem?

— The party is still going full blast at 2 am, but you know it's time to start home. Do you have one last drink before you leave? After all the ups and downs of the night, are you in condition to drive? Would you be able to assess your condition? Would you call your parents to come and pick you up?

— Could you talk to your parents about this kind of night afterward? Beforehand? Would they have let you take the new car? Do they trust you?

SCENARIO #4

You and your friend have just finished off a pizza with the works after seeing the funniest movie of the year. Your friend's sister is coming to pick you up. When she gets there she has two boys in the car with her, and empty beer cans are all over the back seat. She's not too steady on her feet as she gets out to let you into the back seat.

— You hesitate, and she snaps, "Get in or I'm leaving without you." You can smell beer all over her. What thoughts go through your mind in those milliseconds?
— Your friend is already in the car and says, "It's okay. She's a good driver." The boys in the car laugh. How does this affect your decision?
— Would you back away from the car and say, "No, thanks. I'll get another ride"? How would your friend react? Would he/she be your friend after that? Could you talk to him/her about this kind of thing?
— How would you set up a plan beforehand with a parent or a trusted older friend to pick you up no matter what time or where? Whom would you call?

SCENARIO #5

You are on your way home from a party. You didn't drink because you're getting over a strep throat and have been on strong medication for a week. Your best friend is driving and just ran a red light. He/she is drifting into the other lane, and you realize that you may become involved in an accident.

— What is your best course of action? What do you say? What do you do?
— How will your friend react if you decide to do something he/she doesn't agree with?
— How do you carry out your plan?

SCENARIO #6

Your father drinks every Friday and Saturday night. He says it helps him unwind from the hectic week at work. This Friday night your mother calls from a meeting and says she has a flat tire. She wants your father to pick her up. You look at your father, who must have had an extra bad week at work because he's drunker than usual and zonked out on the couch. You have your learner's permit, though.

— What do you say to your mom?
— What would you do about your father?
— How can you help get your mother home?
— How much of this is your responsibility?

SCENARIO #7

Your parents are out for the evening. You've invited three friends over to watch a video and eat up a storm. Two of your friends bring a bottle of vodka. They proceed to drink vodka and orange juice until they are quite drunk. You know that their car keys are in the jacket pocket of one of them. You also know that your parents aren't aware of your little "party."

— What are some choices you have in dealing with your drunk friends?
— Would they understand if you made a decision about their driving home? What decisions could you make?
— Did you help them finish off that bottle of vodka?
— Imagine your parents' coming home when your friends were still there. What would you say to

them, and how would you work out the problem of your friends?
— What would your parents do?

SCENARIO #8

You, your older brother, and several of his friends have been drinking in the park. The friend who drove you there is too drunk to drive. The others are arguing over which one will drive. Then they all turn to you.

"You've hardly had anything to drink. You drive," they say, shoving the keys into your hand. You don't have your license yet, but it's not far to drive home.

— Are you the safest driver there?
— What risks are you taking if you get behind the wheel?
— If you really didn't want to do it, what could you say? What would you do?
— How can you convince older kids, especially those who are drunk and are using impaired judgment, of a different solution to the problem?
— How would you handle your brother?

SCENARIO #9

Your boyfriend has been urging you to drink more with him each time you go out. It does seem more exciting when you go parking with him later if you're both a little high. But lately he's been drinking more, and the two of you have been getting more sexually involved every time.

He says, "Tonight is going to be real special. My parents will be gone all weekend, and we have the whole house to ourselves including my bedroom. I bought your favorite wine too. I know I won't want to take you home, so tell your parents that you're staying over at Annie's tonight."

— How do your feelings for him tie up with your responsibility to yourself?
— Are you ready for total sexual involvement? Is booze a big part of your turn-on? Would you and your boyfriend be responsible about sex if you were both high?
— What options do you have?
— What would you do?

SCENARIO #10

Your mother has set you up to baby-sit at her tennis partner's house. You need the money, and the kids turn out to be well behaved and not too much trouble. Your mother's friend is supposed to drive you home, which is ten miles. When she comes home you notice that she's slurring her words a bit, and she trips on the step into the kitchen. You know that she had been at a party.

— What could you say to this woman?
— How would your mother react if she knew about this? Would you tell on her friend?
— What plans can you work out with your parents so that you don't have to get into a car with someone who has been drinking?
— What do you choose to do?

SCENARIO #11

Basketball practice ran late again. Your father is on the night shift and has gone to work already. Your mother is at a meeting that she couldn't miss, so your older sister must pick you up. Only she's drunk as a skunk when she shows up a half hour after you called her.

To take the bus on this cold night you need 80 cents more than is in your pocket, and walking the four miles home in the dark seems to be your only choice.

- — Can you think of other options?
- — How would you handle your sister?
- — It's night and it's cold. Would it make a difference if it were daytime or warm?

SCENARIO #12

Your ride home from the local hangout left an hour ago. Jack just showed up, and you go over to ask him to take you home. As you get closer you find that Jack smells like a brewery and has a glazed look in his eyes. The only ones left to give you a ride are your ex-girlfriend and the guy who stole her away from you.

- — Is going with Jack your only option?
- — Do pride and bad feelings toward your ex get in the way here?
- — What would you do?

Part of making decisions like the ones presented above is tied in with how you feel about yourself. If you believe in yourself and value your life, that will influence your choices. If your self-esteem is low, you may be easily influenced by others and let them make decisions for you, decisions that may not be in your best interest.

Your friends and peers also influence the choices that you make. Working on your refusal skills may keep you off of center stage when it comes to drinking and driving.

These ideas are taken from a refusal skills training program started by Elliot Herman of Tacoma, Washington. He has trained lots of kids from early elementary grades to high school, from public schools to juvenile detention centers.

Refusal skills encompass five steps:

Step 1. Ask questions (to find out the risk)

How much have you had to drink?

Is this kid reliable who's driving us home after the party?

Will your older sister be sober when she takes us to the concert?

Step 2. Name the trouble (state what could happen to you)

That mean's getting into the car with a drunk driver.

That's driving without a license.

That's dangerous to drink that much.

Step 3. Identify the consequences (define what you stand to lose)

I could lose my license.

My parents would never let me have the car again.

My brother could crash and have a serious accident. We could be badly hurt or even killed.

Step 4. Suggest alternatives (figure out something else to do)

Let's call my mother. She'll pick us up no matter what time it is.

I'd rather sleep here tonight than drive home. I've had too much to drink.

Let's take the bus or walk.

How about leaving this party now? It's getting out of hand, and someone's going to get hurt.

Step 5. Leave (get away from the situation and invite your friends to join you later if they don't come with you now)

If you change your mind, my father will drive you home too. I'll be waiting outside.

I'll be in the kitchen having something to eat. That will pass some time and give me a chance to sober up. You can find me there later if you stay.

I'm going home now, and I'm taking the bus. You can meet me on the corner if you want to come with me.

You may want to practice these five steps as a way to work out answers to the twelve scenarios outlined in this chapter. Formulate answers to give family members or friends when you find yourself in a drinking and driving situation that calls for quick, responsible thinking.

Practicing what to say out loud to your mirror or to another person will help you feel confident when you have to use these steps to stand up to someone who is trying to influence you into doing something dangerous or illegal.

These refusal skills give you a handle to turn the peer pressure around to your advantage, keeping you safe, straight, out of trouble, and alive.

CHAPTER ◇ 8

Parent Pacts

"I went to a Bon Jovi concert in the city two weeks ago," said Joanne, seventeen. "The concert was excellent, but my boyfriend's best friend was so drunk, I don't think he heard much of the music. He was really out of it. And he was driving.

"I was mad at my boyfriend because we had to be in this car with Joe, who was literally all over the road. I was petrified that we would have an accident. But we were two hours away from home. What else could we do?"

Students Against Driving Drunk (SADD) and other organizations promote the idea of a parent pact or contract. A pact is an agreement that both sides can live with and will follow though on when the need arises.

SADD calls it the Contract for Life between a teenager and his or her parents. You and your parent sign a formal written agreement, which acknowledges the potential problem in drinking and driving and states that you both agree to do something about it.

With a parent pact, kids can face a potentially dangerous

situation with confidence, knowing that they have parental support in dealing with it. Often you may feel pressured to get into a car with a drunk driver and, like Joanne, have no alternative lined up.

The contract must also address situations in which the teen is the one who has had too much to drink and is driving and responsible for others.

The other side of the coin is a clause in the contract that the parents agree to the same conditions—that Mom or Dad won't drink and drive or be a passenger in a car with a drunk driver.

As soon as Dave, seventeen, got his license, he and his parents drew up a contract.

"I had heard about this in my health class. At first I thought it was stupid, but after I walked three miles home from a party when my ride decided to stay over because he was just about passed out, I decided to do it. My parents said after that night, 'Why didn't you call us? We would have come to get you.' I guess I was afraid to call them at two in the morning. Besides, I wasn't too straight myself. I didn't want to be grounded. So I walked. Now I don't have to if I get in that mess again."

Joe and his parents sat down and drew up the following contract.

JOE'S AGREEMENT:

I will call you no matter what time it is or where I am if I can't drive because I've been drinking or if my ride is drunk. This doesn't give me permission to get wasted all the time.

JOE'S PARENTS' AGREEMENT:

We agree to come and pick you up when you call us so that you don't drive drunk or get in a car with someone who's been drinking. We reserve the right to discuss the situation the next day. We don't want to punish you, but we don't give you blanket permission to get drunk either.

We also agree not to drink and drive ourselves. We will use the designated driver system and make sure we have safe transportation.

"I wanted my parents to know that I could take care of myself too, so I watch out now and don't take advantage of our contract. I've only had to call them twice, but it was nice to know that I wouldn't get lectured and punished because I made a bad decision. I also know that if I get out of hand I *will* be punished," said Joe.

"You know what was the hardest part?" Joe continued. "Getting my parents to include the part about them not drinking and driving. The old double standard is still alive; you know, do as I say, not as I do?

"My dad said that he has lots of dinner meetings where he drinks and needs to drive home. I asked him why he had to drink at these meetings, and he couldn't give me any better answer than that everyone else did. Then he understood where I was coming from a little better, and I think he has pretty much stopped drinking at those meetings now."

Some teens work out a contract with a relative, a close neighbor, or an older friend if a parent isn't willing or available.

"I live with my father and older sister," Keasha said. "I

could never get my father to sign a contract, so I made one with my sister. She acts like my mother anyway, most of the time. I've called her a couple of times when I was going out with this guy who got drunk every weekend. I was getting into that too. But I was in love, and it seemed the right thing to do at the time.

"My sister tried to break us up, but that only made me want to be with him more. That finally changed when I got bored with just sitting in this other guy's apartment drinking all Friday, Saturday, and Sunday. But if I didn't have the agreement with my sister to come and get me when I couldn't get home, I probably would have been in Eddie's car when he ran off the road last month."

Working out a contract enables teens and parents to open the door to deeper trust and communication. It also lets kids see that parents too can have similar problems. Equal responsibilities and no double standard are the goals of a parent pact.

Contracts and pacts can allow teens to talk about their fears, their life, and keep a cloak of parental protection around them at a time when they often resist parental interference.

It also gives parents a chance to talk about their worries and concerns and to show their love and feelings of responsibility in a different light.

But there also has to be a real effort on both sides to keep it a responsible agreement.

"We didn't write our contract down or anything," said Maria, seventeen. "But I know I can call my parents when I have been drinking or if I have no safe ride home. They won't hang up on me or scream and yell, but I also know that if I go too far or drink too much there will be consequences. Mom especially works on me about drinking and all the problems it can bring. They want me to wait until

I'm twenty-one, and the more we talk about it, the less I drink. Then I don't have to call them to come get me."

If a parent pact is regarded as permission to get wasted and then call Mom or Dad to bail you out, the agreement is worthless. The contract is your agreement to act responsibly so that your parents can trust you more. That is the goal. Because the more trust you earn, the more freedom you'll get. Isn't that worth it?

CHAPTER ◇ 9

Deterrence, Intervention, Prevention

Drunk drivers are of all kinds. There is no way to stereotype the typical DUI (Driving Under the Influence) or DWI (Driving While Intoxicated) offender.

Seventeen-year-old Matt and his friends were celebrating their high school football team's victory over a cross-town rival. Chugging some beers in the parking lot after the game was cause for much hilarity and feelings of camaraderie. Matt, his younger brother, and two friends took off in his car to meet the others at the local Pizza Palace. They never arrived.

Matt didn't handle that last curve on Bartley Road too

well. His car skidded out of control and slammed into a telephone pole. It was the first time he had ever had an accident. It was the last time for his younger brother and two friends. They were killed instantly.

Mary was thirty-five. She had been having some personal and emotional problems, and stopped off at a local bar after work one Friday night. One drink led to another until she realized it was getting late and she had to get home to feed her cats. She never got there.

On the way, Mary fell asleep at the wheel (or maybe she passed out), and her car went off the road into a shallow pond. Luckily for her, a passerby pulled her from her car before she drowned. She was convicted of DUI and lost her license for six months.

Don was forty-nine. He had two previous convictions for DUI over the past four years. He had spent time in jail, paid fines, lost his license several times, and even gone through driver retraining and an alcohol rehabilitation program.

Don wasn't deterred. He continued to drink and drive. He figured that since he had never had a serious accident he didn't have to change his ways. He liked to drink. He liked to drive. No one was going to stop him from doing either. Tragically, his decision didn't affect only him. The last time he drank and then got behind the wheel, he seriously injured nineteen-year-old Pam and killed her three-year-old niece Tanya. Don didn't make it out of the wreck alive either.

* * *

Drinking drivers range from the inexperienced at both drinking and driving to alcoholics who are incapable of considering the welfare of others. It is not only the Skid Row bum types who cause accidents. All kinds of people of all ages and across all social classes and walks of life are arrested and convicted of DUI. And even more do it but don't get caught. Not getting caught doesn't make it any less potentially dangerous.

DUI drivers (convicted or not) share common traits. They misuse alcohol, make poor decisions using impaired judgment, and don't realize how much they are affected by what they drink. So laws are passed to try to reduce the frightening death and injury statistics caused by DUI criminals.

There is no one single solution to the problem. It's nice, but somewhat naive, to think that suspending someone's license is enough to stop him or her from ever getting behind the wheel less than sober. Sadly, some people continue to drive even after their license is revoked.

Shouldn't time in jail be enough to scare people away from DUI? The number of repeat offenders who have been incarcerated show that it does not.

The problem of driving while intoxicated has many aspects, and that is why the several states use a combination of approaches in combating this life-threatening menace.

The American Automobile Association (AAA) Foundation for Traffic Safety has outlined a three-pronged approach to what it calls the "number one traffic safety problem by far today—drunk driving." The approach encompasses *deterrence*, *intervention*, and *prevention*.

DETERRENCE

The deterrence aspect has evolved into tougher laws with more severe penalties designed to discourage people who use alcohol and then drive. Those who work in the field agree that tougher laws and more severe penalties do make people think twice to lessen the chances of being caught and punished. Tougher laws do lower the rates of arrest and conviction.

Over the past ten years the majority of states have tightened up their DUI laws. Publicity has been instituted on a national level. Publicizing penalties and offenders has also become a method of deterrence on the local level.

Jail sentences are another way to deter intoxicated drivers. Many teens and adults who have spent from a few hours to several days in jail vow never to do that again. However, jail has only a short-term effect on some people, and with sentences being commuted to probation or community service, jail loses its sting as a deterrent.

INTERVENTION

Intervention encompasses reeducation, retraining, and rehabilitating drivers convicted of DUI.

Almost every state has mandated reeducation/rehabilitation for first-time DUI offenders. In most high schools teenagers take driver education theory class, usually in tenth or eleventh grade. They may receive instruction at fifteen, sixteen, or even as late as seventeen for some kids. In these classes, *how* to drive is the main focus.

If you are arrested for DUI, you will most likely be assigned to driver reeducation. "But I already know how to drive!" you say. "I only drank a little and had a fender-bender. I don't need this program."

Actually, you have no choice. The programs combine alcohol education and driver retraining. The thrust is to convince you of the dangers of driving when you've had too much to drink. They are also designed to help you develop future coping and decision-making skills to avoid what you were arrested for in the first place.

As much as the facts have been publicized, most people don't realize that a usual serving of beer (12 ounces), a glass of wine (4 to 5 ounces), and a shot of vodka in orange juice are *equal* in how they intoxicate you. The programs also reeducate you with information that you need to keep in mind, such as:

- How many drinks you consume and of what strength.
- How much time after "safe" or "legal" drinking must elapse before you drive.
- How your weight affects how drunk you get.
- How your state of mind and physical being affect your drinking.
- How the amount and what you have eaten before and while you drink influences your level of intoxication.
- How other drugs in your body (including antihistamines for allergies, cough syrup, and other over-the-counter drugs) combine with the alcohol.

Remember that alcohol is not digested. It goes directly to the bloodstream.

Your brain works with a rich supply of blood, so alcoholic drinks can feel as if they go straight to your head. You need to be aware of your BAC (blood alcohol content), which impairs your judgment and physical coordination. You need to "know when to say when" (to quote yet another media promotion for beer).

The programs mentioned above reeducate you and drive home these facts, so that you have the information you need to make safe judgments and good decisions about future situations you may face.

Alcohol rehabilitation programs usually involve taking the DUI offender to a treatment center to face and deal with the drinking problem. The first step, which is also the hardest step, is admitting that you have a problem. Having a problem doesn't mean that you drink every day or even every weekend. But if alcohol and drinking play an important part in your life, and you drink to deal with life's ups and downs, a rehab program can help you redirect your life.

Intervention programs such as retraining and rehab are fairly successful, especially for the younger DUI offenders. You have had fewer years in which to become a heavy drinker, are more stable physically and mentally, and can be at a point of your life where you welcome intervention and a chance to redirect your life in a better, healthier direction.

These programs are not just an easy way out. They usually are required in addition to other penalties, not in place of them. You still have to pay the court-imposed fines, and you have to pay for the program itself. In many cases your follow-up probation may mandate your continuance at AA (Alcoholics Anonymous) meetings or involvement with other social agencies.

A recent law instituted in California has created a program to show young DUI offenders what may be in store for them if they don't change their drinking and driving habits. These teens and young adults tour hospitals and institutions where auto accident victims are treated or where victims are hooked up to life-support systems just to stay alive.

They may even go to the county morgue (where bodies are kept before they are sent to funeral homes) or to the medical examiner's autopsy room (where doctors operate on dead people to determine the cause of death). The offenders see the victims of fatal drunk driving accidents up close and in person. First-time offenders must attend this pilot program or spend time in jail.

New Jersey is working on a similar program to "scare" teenagers and young adults who have been convicted of DUI.

These intervention programs are designed to redirect those already in trouble and to reduce the chances of repeat DUI crimes. If even a small percentage can be made to change the present course of their life, the programs are considered successful. Unfortunately, new offenders account for 85 to 90 percent of the continuing drunk driving problem.

PREVENTION

Prevention programs are another important phase of combatting the killer on the road. They are designed to educate the public, starting with the very young, to encourage safe drinking habits. Since the leading cause of teenage death is accidents (60 percent of *fatal* accidents are alcohol-related), safety education and alcohol information are aimed at preschool and elementary school children and up.

The media are starting to move away from from the drink, drink, drink mentality of beer commercials, but kids still see famous athletes downing can after can of their favorite name-brand brew. Even though Spuds McKenzie "knows when to say when," he's still the party animal, popular and loved, that kids aspire to become.

Because beer and wine commercials are allowed on TV,

but not hard liquor advertising, kids think that wine coolers and light beer are not as intoxicating as vodka, rum, or whiskey. The ads still portray drinking as the only way to celebrate, to "party," or to have happy, romantic times. Have you ever seen a commercial with baseball players drinking and discussing how the beer they are guzzling reduces their judgment and driving skills, or saying that they are not driving tonight so they won't cause an accident? That stuff doesn't sell beer.

The AAA Foundation for Traffic Safety promotes a comprehensive program that integrates deterrence, intervention, and prevention. These measures require a coordinated effort from the police, the court system, teachers and educators, judges, prosecutors, motor vehicle officials, and lawmakers.

According to the Foundation, this integration should include and promote:

- Laws that will result in DUI convictions without plea bargaining (taking a lesser guilty plea rather than DUI).
- Driver reducation and alcohol rehabilitation programs.
- Closer monitoring of repeat DUI criminals to keep them off the road until they are determined fit to drive safely.
- Public education and information programs that promote drunk driving as unacceptable.
- K-12 alcohol and traffic safety programs in schools.
- An evaluation procedure to measure effectiveness of the above in order to continue a safe, effective, coordinated effort to make our highways safe.

CHAPTER ◇ 10

THE LAW

Driving after drinking is a gamble. Okay, you made it home safely the last time. What? You don't remember much of the drive, but the next morning your parents' car was parked in the driveway and you woke up in your own bed? No harm, right?

What about the next time? Or the next? Or when you get in the car with your best friend who chugged a six-pack of beer in the last hour and a half? Feel lucky? Are you happy to push the odds?

DUI (Driving Under the Influence) is one of the biggest gambles you can take in your life. If you went to Atlantic City or Las Vegas with the odds of DUI arrest, you'd do very well. Over 50 percent of all fatal accidents happen when a driver has been drinking. Over 40 percent of drivers killed on the road are intoxicated when the accident happens.

The National Safety Council promotes ROAD (Risks, Odds, and Decisions) as an informational program about the risks a driver takes when drinking. The following from the ROAD program is important information that you need to consider.

ARREST!

With the strong push to keep drunk drivers off the nation's highways, many towns and cities have strengthened their police enforcement of DUI checks. During holiday seasons checkpoints are set up, stopping drivers randomly to determine whether they've been drinking. At other times police continue to pull over random or suspicious drivers. With the strong laws enacted in every state over the past five to ten years and nationally, much police effort is being made to keep drunk drivers off the roads.

If you or your friend are pulled over on suspicion of DUI, you'll be asked to take a breath test to assess the alcohol concentration in your body. If you refuse or fail the test, your driver's license is revoked for thirty days or more before you even see a courtroom.

Hey, not fair! you say. If I refuse to take the test, how can I be guilty until I prove my innocence? How can I prove my innocence after that? It's like being framed.

It may seem that they've got you coming and going. With the severity of the drunk driving laws, you *have* to take that test to prove you are innocent if you really are. Maybe you see it as losing your freedom, but when you get behind the wheel of a potentially lethal weapon and you're not sober enough to drive, you are stepping all over the freedom of others to have a safe ride. When you crash and kill another person—well, taking another's life is taking away the ultimate freedom.

Being arrested (failing the test for intoxication) is serious business. And expensive. Lawyer's fees, fines, and time in jail are the outcomes that you gamble against. You lose.

CONVICTION!

You appear in court. Bam! The gavel sounds out the finality of your sentence.

Sentence? You mean like long-term jail and criminal stuff? But I'm not a criminal.

Yes, you are. DUI is a criminal activity. Once you are convicted, you face the consequences.

FINES!

Each state has its own laws, but for DUI you pay fines ranging from $250 to $1,000 for your first conviction.

JAIL!

Spending 48 hours or up to a year in jail is also a penalty for a first-time DUI. Some states allow you to do community service work in lieu of jail time, such as working in your town or community on rebuilding, cleaning up, helping others.

REHABILITATION!

Enrolling in a driver improvement program is usually required for DUI offenders. Many states mandate that you undergo an alcohol rehabilitation program and assessment to help you straighten out your drinking problem.

PROBATION!

Instead of jail time, a few states require probation. That means that your behavior and life-style will be monitored for a specific period of time, possibly one to three years.

Your probation officer may check with your family, your school, your teachers, and your employer to make sure you are staying straight and out of trouble. You are responsible to report to your probation officer once a month or at an appointed specific time.

LICENSE REVOCATION!

Remember how long you waited to get your license? Those days and weeks of longing and practicing in your parents' car getting ready to drive? The ultimate privilege! The ultimate freedom! The *ultimate responsibility*.

Get a DUI conviction and kiss your license good-bye for at least a couple of months, perhaps for as long as a year. Good-bye privilege. Good-bye freedom. You didn't measure up to the responsibility.

FINANCIAL PROBLEMS!

Talk to a lawyer sometime and ask him/her to estimate the fee to help you fight a DUI arrest and court procedure. Add to that the fine you will have to pay if and when convicted, and you probably will find out that your savings account won't cover the expenses.

FAMILY PROBLEMS!

Being arrested and convicted of DUI will not make you popular in your family. The worry, stress, and anxiety that you, your parents, and any other family members undergo can be unbelievable. Arguments, accusations, denials, and breakups are possible outcomes. Nowadays, newspapers are reporting the names of those arrested and convicted of DUI. The reactions of people in your community are hard to predict. Guilt and shame cannot always be hidden away or ignored.

LOSS OF JOB!

No car, no transportation. No wheels, no job. Employers can't rely on you if you are not able to get to work, whether it's a part-time job after school or full-time employment. License revocation can mean a quick end to your job, especially one in which you are required to drive. There goes your paycheck, bringing on more financial woes.

Finding a new job may be difficult with a DUI conviction on your record. Most job applications ask if you have ever been convicted of a crime. DUI is a crime. Few employers are willing to hire someone who seemingly has an alcohol problem.

But I only made one mistake! Do I have to pay for it forever? Sometimes it seems that way. It certainly is a hard lesson to learn. But it is also one that could have been avoided in the first place.

"He's a drunk."

"She almost killed that young couple."

Social stigma. There's been too much about drunk driving in the media for the American public to go soft on DUI offenders. This behavior is not acceptable in the mind of the public, and you will evoke very little sympathy as a drunk driver.

The consequences of DUI outlined above are for first-time offenders. Things get even more serious if you are convicted a second time within several years. (Some state laws encompass convictions within three years; others are five, a few are seven, some ten.) A third conviction keeps piling on the jail time and fines.

It's a different story if you are convicted of DUI and cause injury or death to another person. You'll spend years in prison, pay heavy fines, and lose your license for quite a few years. Add to that the guilt you'll feel for hurting, crippling, or killing another human being and you've got a Pandora's box of consequences for something you could have avoided in the first place.

The following are randomly selected states and their penalties and consequences for a DUI arrest and conviction. Check with your local police department or state motor vehicle agency for your own state laws. States are tightening up these laws every year, so it's important for you to know the current law and what you risk when you drink and drive.

ALABAMA (1987)
BAC .10

1st offense:

Imprisonment up to a year and/or $250 to $1,000 fine. Mandatory 90-day license revocation. Court-referred DUI program.

2nd offense within 5 years:

Imprisonment (including hard labor) not more than a year; mandatory minimum 48 consecutive hours or community service for not less than 20 days; $500 to $2,000 fine. One-year revocation of license.

3rd or subsequent offenses within 5 years:

Mandatory 60 days imprisonment; $1,000 to $5,000 fine. Mandatory 3-year license revocation.

CALIFORNIA (1988)
BAC .10

1st offense:

Imprisonment 4 days to 6 months (may be served weekends); $390 to $1,000 fine. Six-month license revocation.

2nd offense within 7 years:

Imprisonment 90 days to 1 year; $390 to $1,000 fine. One-year license revocation.

3rd offense within 7 years:

Imprisonment 120 days to 1 year; $390 to $1,000 fine. Three-year license revocation.

DISTRICT OF COLUMBIA (1987)
BAC .10

1st offense:

Fine no more than $300 and/or 90 days imprisonment.

2nd offense within 15 years:

Fine no more than $5,000 and/or up to 1 year imprisonment.

3rd offense within 15 years:

Fine no more than $10,000 and/or up to 1 year imprisonment.

All offenses:

Mandatory license revocation.

FLORIDA (1987)
BAC .10

1st offense:

Imprisonment up to 6 months (9 months if BAC is .20); $250 to $500 fine ($500 to $1,000 if BAC is .20). License revocation 180 days to 1 year. Community service 50 hours. Up to 1 year probation.

2nd offense within 5 years:

Imprisonment 10 days to 9 months; $500 to $1,000 fine ($1,000 to $2,000 if BAC is .20). Minimum 5-year license revocation.

3rd offense within 5 years:

Imprisonment 30 days to 12 months; $1,000 to $2,500 fine ($2,000 minimum if BAC is .20). License revocation 10 years for 3rd offense within 10 years.

All offenses:

Substance abuse course and/or alcohol evaluation and treatment program at court's discretion.

4th or subsequent conviction:

Third-degree felony.

ILLINOIS (1988)
BAC .10

1st offense:

Class A misdemeanor. Less than 1 year imprisonment and/or up to $1,000 fine. Driving privilege revoked. Professional evaluation of alcohol problem prior to final sentencing.

2nd or subsequent offense within 5 years:

Mandatory minimum 48 consecutive hours of imprisonment or minimum 10 days community service in addition to any other penalties imposed. No probation or suspension of sentence.

*Note: Class 4 felony is charged if violation was proximate cause of bodily harm or permanent disability or disfigurement to another.

MAINE (1986)
BAC .10

1st offense:

Class D crime. Imprisonment 48 hours to less than 1 year; $300 to $1,000 fine. License revocation 90 days.

2nd offense:

Class D crime. Imprisonment 7 days to less than 1 year; $500 to $1,000 fine. License revocation 1 year.

3rd or subsequent offense within 6 years:

Class D crime. Imprisonment 30 days to less than 1 year; $750 to $1,000 fine. License revocation 2 years.

All offenses:

Court cannot suspend minimum fine, minimum period of imprisonment, or license revocation.

MINNESOTA (1988)
BAC .10

1st offense:

Imprisonment no more than 10 days and/or fine of no more than $700. Not less than 30-day revocation of license.

2nd or subsequent offense within 5 years (gross misdemeanor):

Imprisonment no more than 1 year and/or fine no more than $3,000. Not less than 90-day license revocation and certification of successfully completed treatment or rehabilitation.

3rd offense within 5 years (gross misdemeanor):

Same as 2nd offense but not less than 1-year license revocation.

4th or subsequent offense:

Same as 2nd but no less than 2-year license revocation.

NEW HAMPSHIRE (1987)
BAC .10

1st offense:

Imprisonment 90 days. Up to $1,000 fine. License revocation 2 years.

2nd or subsequent offense within 7 years (misdemeanor):

Imprisonment not less than 10 consecutive days. Fine up to $1,000. Revocation of license 3 years. (If more than one prior offense, license revoked indefinitely.)

NEW JERSEY (1988)
BAC .10

1st offense:

Mandatory: $250 to $500 fine; 6-month to 1-year license revocation, discretionary imprisonment not to exceed 30 days, and 12 to 48 hours detainment in an Intoxicated Driver Resource Center at a charge of $25 a day.

2nd offense:

Mandatory: $500 to $1,000 fine, 30 days community service, 2-year license revocation, imprisonment of not less than 48 consecutive hours nor more than 90 days.

3rd offense:

Mandatory: $1,000 fine, 10-year license revocation, 180 days imprisonment. A $100 surcharge to be deposited in Drunk Driving Enforcement Fund.

All offenses:

Complete a D.M.V. Alcohol Countermeasure Screening and Evaluation Program.

An auto insurance surcharge of $1,000 a year for three years is assessed on 1st and 2nd offenses; surcharge on 3rd offense is $1,500 a year for 3 years.

OKLAHOMA (1988)
BAC .10

1st offense (misdemeanor):

Imprisonment 10 days to 1 year. Fine no more than $1,000. License revocation 90 days.

2nd or subsequent offense (felony):

Imprisonment 1 to 5 years. No more than $2,500 fine. License revocation 90 days.

TEXAS (1988)
BAC .10

1st offense:

Fine $100 to $2,000. Imprisonment 72 hours to 2 years.

2nd offense:

Fine $300 to $2,000. Imprisonment 15 days to 2 years.

3rd or subsequent offense:

Fine $500 to $2,000. Imprisonment 30 days to 2 years or 60 days to 5 years.

WISCONSIN (1987)
BAC .10

1st offense:

Fine $150 to $300; 6-month license revocation.

2nd offense within 5 years:

Fine $300 to $1,000; imprisonment 5 days to 6 months; 1-year license revocation.

3rd offense within 5 years:

Fine $600 to $2,000; imprisonment 30 days to 1 year; 2-year license revocation.

REFUSAL TO TAKE BREATH TEST

Many states have laws governing the refusal to cooperate in taking the breath test. New Jersey is one example:

1st offense: Mandatory $250 to $500 fine and 6-month license revocation.

2nd offense: Mandatory $250 to $500 fine and 2-year license revocation.

Many states have subsequent penalties for driving after the court has revoked your license. They are usually a mandatory fine of an additional $500 to $1,000, more months on the revoked list, and jail time.

The laws are getting stiffer every day. In many cases punishments and penalties are mandatory. The days of the suspended sentence, at least for DUI offenses, are gone. Society is demanding retribution from people who use their cars as potential lethal weapons because of intoxication.

CHAPTER ◇ 11

Protection

If you are driving, a passenger in a car, or riding your bike on the road, there are ways you can spot an impaired or a drunk driver. Knowing how to recognize these signals and react to them may lessen your chances of being involved in an alcohol-related accident.

A person swerving or not driving a normally straight path on the correct side of the road is a driver from whom you want to stay away. He or she may be driving on the shoulder or may cross into the opposite lane before pulling back to the correct side.

Misjudging turns, either by unusually wide turns or by abrupt or illegal turns is another sure sign. In a recent accident, a sixty-year-old drunk woman made a left turn into the northbound lane of a divided highway. Although she was not going very fast, she crashed into a compact car driven by a twenty-year-old woman who was five months pregnant. The young woman and her baby died. The drunk woman had minor injuries.

An impaired driver may also respond slowly to traffic signals, straddle or drive on the center line, or speed up or slow down for no reason. Forgetting to put on headlights and tailgating are other warning signs.

"I was standing on a corner waiting for the light to change," Shannon, age twelve, said. "This guy drives up and he's driving with his head out the window, like he can't see except his windshield looked clean to me."

A sure bet is that this driver has had too much to drink and is trying to "sober up" as he drives. Unfortunately, his attention is on keeping his head out the window, not his eyes on the road. Watch out.

Okay. You are driving with your learner's permit, and your friend who is a licensed driver is in the passenger seat next to you. Ahead is a flashy new TransAm but it seems to be having trouble staying on the right side of the road. Every once in a while it shoulders the road and then pulls back toward the center line.

What do you do?

Instead of driving up closer to see the car and investigate what may be happening with it, hang back and maintain a safe following distance (one car length for each ten mph you are driving). Stay away from that car and its driver.

You know those blinking-light intersections that are so easy to cruise though? Even if you have the yellow blinker as opposed to the red blinker, you can slow down almost to a stop and check out the cross road. Impaired drivers forget to use their turn signals or are not able to judge stopping distances. Be safe, not sorry.

Look out! Someone is coming at you over the center line! Sound your horn, flash your lights, and pull over to the right. Always make sure you are seatbelted in, and lock the doors for safety.

Get to a telephone, or if you have a CB in your car, use it! Call the police and report the drunk driver. As best you can, give a description of the car, its license number, and a location and direction in which it was headed. Even though you are shook up, do the best you can. The police can follow up on your information. You could save someone else's life.

"I was at a 7–11 one night," Krisann said. "These four girls were in there laughing and giggling. I knew they were drunk.

"When they got in their car and took off, I wrote down the license number and called the police. My friend said I was ratting on them, but my father had been hurt by a drunk driver years ago, and our family doesn't fool around. I don't know if the police did anything or not, but at least I did."

THE DESIGNATED DRIVER

Another way you can protect yourself is to use the designated driver system. The designated driver is someone your group chooses to drive on an occasion when you others will be drinking. One person volunteers and is responsible for driving the rest of you home safely.

In Sweden and England, where this idea started, designated drivers put their car keys in their empty glass so that no one serves them liquor.

Having a designated driver acknowledges that people do drink but that everyone can be resonsible for safe trips home. At the next party someone else takes his or her turn, and the group rotates the responsibility.

"Yeah, but I don't trust this one guy in our group," eighteen-year-old Joel said. "He only volunteered once, and we trusted that he would stay sober but he didn't. We never let him do it again, and now we end up taxiing him home drunk every time. It's like we're his baby-sitters or something."

That kind of irresponsible person makes things hard on the whole group. You have to be able to trust your friends and take turns. Maybe leaving this guy out a few times will change his ways; if not, at least you'll be free of being his keeper.

"I kind of like being the DD (designated driver)," Mickey said. "That way I don't have to drink, which I don't like to do anyway, and it gets me off the hook when kids keep putting beers in my hand."

The DD doesn't have to be one who doesn't drink at all. A driver having one or two drinks over the course of three or four hours can be a choice. But if there's a better, safer choice, take it. But it must be someone you can trust that when she says she hasn't had anything to drink, it's the truth.

People who say, "Well, I haven't had *that* much to drink. I can still drive," can still be a dangerous choice. The social drinker as well as the alcoholic can be a menace on the road. The sixteen- to twenty-four-year-old driving group still accounts for more than one third of alcohol-related car accidents. Social drinkers can be impaired because their judgment, reaction time, and coordination are affected to some degree. The safest way to drive home from a party is straight-up sober.

CHAPTER ◇ 12

The Aftermath of Drinking and Driving

Laura was seventeen when it happened. She was a high school track star, in top shape, and enjoying her successes in competitions and in school.

Two weeks before the accident, coaches from a top university had offered Laura an athletic scholarship. All her hard work, training, and studying were paying off.

"We weren't even at a major party—just eight of us girls together sipping wine coolers and giggling. No big drinking binge. Nobody was wasted or anything like that." Laura's dark eyes were sad as she spoke.

"On the way home Marta was driving and I was in the back seat right behind her. We had just passed a park where our boyfriends hang out, and we were beeping the horn and yelling. I guess we were a little high and not paying attention."

Laura gave a shudder as if the memory of that night sent a chill up her spine. "Marta ran the stop sign at the next block. We didn't go far into the intersection, and she slammed on her brakes as soon as she could. But we skidded about five feet more into the middle of the road. The car coming on our left veered off trying to avoid us, but as we slammed to a skidding stop he crashed right into the side of the car where I was sitting.

"Anyway, to cut things short, Marta was in the hospital for a while and still has trouble with her back. Me? I have a pin in my leg where the bone was crushed, and there went my college scholarship."

Laura shook her head. "I thought it was the end of the world. My world, anyway. After all the therapy on my leg, I missed six months of college, and now I have to wait out the entire year. I'm starting to run again, but I'll never be able to compete on a college level. My life will never be the way I had planned. I had to change my dreams a lot, and that was hard."

Lots of teenagers drink as Laura and her friends did. Some wine coolers or a few beers and no harm done, right? But even this so-called social drinking affects your ability to drive. Add to a small amount of alcohol the inexperience of young drivers, and you could be headed on a collision course.

Scott wasn't as lucky as Laura.

"When I was eighteen, I was on top of the world! I had a good-looking girlfriend, a part-time job, and as soon as I graduated I was going to work full time for my uncle framing houses. I love working with my hands building stuff. My uncle was making unbelievable money, and he needed my help. I was set."

Scott told this story from a motorized wheelchair that works on a sip-and-puff control device. He is paralyzed from the neck down because of irreparable damage done to his spine in not one but two car crashes.

"The first accident I had wasn't so bad, ya know? I only

had to wear a neck brace because I messed up my back a little. Because I failed the drunk test I was convicted of drunk driving and lost my license for thirty days, paid a fine of $300, and had to go to a driver training course."

As he choked up a bit, Scott's mother came over to hold the tissue while he blew his nose, his useless hands lying in his lap.

"Even with the driving classes and all that scary stuff they used to try to make us change our habits, I didn't learn. I knew better. I figured I had already used up my share of bad luck, and it wouldn't happen to me again, right?

"Wrong. No sooner had I gotten my license back than I got drunk with my friends and crashed again. That's how I landed in this chair. I really lost my license for good," Scott added ironically.

"I'll never drive again, walk again, write again, or do much of anything for myself again. If I knew then what I know now, I would have listened. Kids should spend time in a chair without using their hands if they want to know what could happen to them mixing drinking and driving."

For some young drivers and their passengers fate is worse than what Laura and Scott suffered. Every year over 25,000 people in the United States suffer severe head injuries because of drunk driving.

In the Midwest, Randi was a straight-A student and president of her senior class. A seventeen-year-old drunk driver changed her forever in 1987. Injuries from that accident left Randi with broken bones in her leg and a bruised head that put her in a coma when she smashed into the windshield.

Randi's brain stem had a tiny but damaging wound. While she was comatose Randi's athletic body was transformed into a crippled quadriplegic whose hands and feet are contracted and spastic.

After five months in a coma and two years of continuous therapy in a hospital, Randi is learning to speak again and recover her memory. She will never leave her wheelchair.

Severe head trauma can cause you to be in a coma, lose your memory, create gaps in your knowledge, and make you very dependent on other people. Statistics show that the typical victim of severe head trauma is a young man between fifteen and twenty-five years old. Of these young guys, barely 5 percent (that's five out of every 100 victims) can live a normal life after their accident.

Many of these head trauma victims have to be cared for by their families. Others wind up in institutions for years or the rest of their lives. The National Head Injury Foundation estimates that the cost of critical care for a coma victim in a hospital trauma unit can run $150,000 for the first few months. The cost of care for the rest of his or her life can run well over $4 million.

Many insurance companies cap medical benefits at $1 million, leaving no provision for rehabilitation that could take years if and when a victim emerges from the coma. Average families have to muster courage and face incredible odds in caring for their family member who is a coma/head trauma victim.

Mental health and special education institutions such as those run by the Devereux Foundation in Philadelphia and in Santa Barbara, California, provide programs for head trauma patients whose injuries leave them unable to function. The patients who are involved in these programs because of drunk driving represent up to two thirds of the total patients.

Your brain can take everyday bumps without too much

damage. But when you hit a windshield or car frame at even what you think is a slow speed, you can do irreparable damage to your brain. Besides the obvious advice not to drink and drive, another way to avoid brain trauma is to wear your seatbelt.

Statistics complied by Patrick O'Malley, PhD, and Lloyd Johnston, PhD, at the Institute for Social Research, University of Michigan, show how today's teens feel about using seatbelts. They presented testimony at hearings before the National Commission Against Drunk Driving and the National Highway Traffic Safety Administration at Fort Worth, Texas, in March, 1988.

These doctors reported the results of a survey of 17,000 seniors in their Monitoring the Future project.

Percentage of Seniors Using Seatbelts When Driving

	1986	1987
Never, Seldom	43.2	36.7
Always	25.0	33.0

Percentage of Seniors Using Seatbelts When Riding as Passengers in Front Seat

	1986	1987
Never, Seldom	46.6	39.0
Always	22.0	30.1

Drs. O'Malley and Johnston also reported that the tendency to wear a seatbelt is distinctly lower among the kids who reported driving after drinking. Of the seniors who drove after having five or more drinks, only one third were likely to buckle up when driving compared to nondrinking drivers (12% vs. 38%). Clouded judgment plays a part in that factor.

Although, according to this national survey, it appears that teenagers are using seatbelts more, still too many do not either most of the time or at all.

If you are in a car accident without having your seatbelt buckled, you run a high risk for:

1. Cracking your head into the frame of the car, causing brain trauma.
2. Hitting your head and face into the windshield.
3. Shattering the windshield as your head and face smash through the shards of glass.

Patricia Waller of the Highway Safety Research Center at the University of North Carolina did an extensive analysis of over one million accidents. Her research shatters the myth that you're more relaxed when you're drunk and thus don't get hurt as badly as when you're sober.

The driver who has been drinking is more vulnerable to injury or sudden death because of alcohol's effect on the nervous system, which includes the brain and spinal cord. If your brain is injured, the alcohol will worsen your situation because it increases cerebral swelling.

Know the risks. Weigh the consequences. Make your plans about how you will deal with these kinds of situations. It could mean the difference between life and death.

CHAPTER ◇ 13

Families Who Grieve

The following letter was written to the editor of a newspaper and printed in remembrance of a beloved daughter.

School is out and it's time for summer fun, but my daughter, Becky King, won't enjoy the beach, or her friends, or anything else, ever again. She would have celebrated her nineteenth birthday on July 6. She probably would have gone to the beach, perhaps meeting her friends on the boardwalk later.

Mr. Drunk Driver, how are you going to be spending Becky's birthday this year? I'll be going to the cemetery and putting flowers on her grave. I'm saving a little money out of each paycheck for her headstone. That's the last birthday present I'll ever be able to give her.

The first gift I gave Becky was the gift of life. Did you know, Mr. Drunk Driver, that Becky was premature? Learning was a constant struggle for her, but she never gave up. As her eighteenth birthday approached, she was so excited about becoming "an adult." She had plans, Mr. Drunk Driver. She had hopes and dreams. Becky got to be "an adult" for a whole twenty-nine days, and then you took all that away from her, Mr. Drunk Driver.

Just before midnight last July 30, you had an accident. You broke your ankle, Mr. Drunk Driver, but Becky arrived at the hospital in a coma. The first-aiders, paramedics, emergency room staff, and doctors did everything humanly possible to keep Becky alive, but the damage was simply too great. After clinging to life for six days, at 3:30 pm, Friday, August 5, 1988, Becky King died.

I have forgiven you for the accident, Mr. Drunk Driver, because I know that you never put Becky on your motorcycle with the intention of killing her. But I have a serious problem with the fact that you knew you had no motorcycle license, or insurance, and were revoked in two states, and you knew you had two prior drunk-driving convictions before that night!

Becky was God's child before she was mine, and He has taken her back, and her pain and suffering are over. But my pain and suffering, and that of my family, will continue forever. And you, Mr. Drunk Driver, will have to carry the burden of what you did to Becky for the rest of your life.

Why am I writing this letter? Because I want teens and young adults to live and enjoy their summer. Please don't drink and drive, and please don't be a drunk driver's passenger!

Mr. Drunk Driver, how are you going to be spending Becky's birthday this year?

Pat O'Connor
(Becky King's Mom)

Becky's family will never be the same again. Lives were shattered by a drunk driver who had been *convicted twice* for DUI and had lost his license. Drunk drivers don't think about the hurt they can cause, physically and emotionally, to so many people. Their judgment is impaired, and no one else on the road or on the sidewalks is safe.

Fourteen-year-old Allison was walking down a country road with a friend when a pick-up truck came speeding up behind her. It happened so fast that Allison never had a chance. Her friend jumped out of the way of the swerving vehicle and yelled to Ally, who turned around just in time to see the truck smash into her.

The driver lurched on down the road, swerving as he went, while Allison's friend reached out, horrified, to touch Allison's broken body.

"I still get nightmares," Ally's friend said. "My counselor has helped me a lot, but I think I'll never get over that one split second when I could have pulled her out of the way or something. It was horrible." She covered her eyes and began to cry.

The driver who killed Allison was never caught, even though a description of the truck was given to the police. Was the driver drunk? That could never be proved, but the description of the hit-and-run suggests that strongly. Was the driver even aware of what he or she did?

Allison's friend is still having trouble getting over the accident she witnessed, even though it's been almost two years.

"For a while, I was so numb that I couldn't believe it. Ally was there one second and we were talking about her boyfriend, and the next second she was ten feet down the road, lying there all bloody and still. I hate that driver so much."

More lives forever altered by a drunk driver.

"My brother Paul was out drinking with his friends," said Karen, now nineteen. "It was a few years ago when the drinking age around here was eighteen. They had been bar-hopping, and none of the bartenders refused to serve them, I guess." She took a deep breath.

"Anyway, they got pretty drunk and Paul got into his friend's car. This 'friend' was in no condition to drive and should have known it. They crashed into a parked car on my brother's side. Paul was crushed and killed instantly. His friend got a bruised rib and walked away from the accident." Karen brushed her dark hair out of her eyes as they filled up with tears.

"Well, my parents and I didn't think that the punishment for the driver was strong enough, so we got petitions signed and had all kinds of red tape put up around the case. Nobody would give us information such as the police records or the court's investigation. We wanted justice served, and no one would help us. My brother was dead, and his killer walked away!"

Karen and her family poured two years of effort into trying to get a stiffer punishment for the driver. They also instituted lawsuits against the bars and bartenders who had continued to serve Paul and his friends after they were drunk.

"My psychologist is trying to help me put this behind me now. Five years is a long time to be consumed by hatred. My life has been a mess since I was fourteen. I never had a normal teenage life because I felt that with Paul dead I had no right to a happy life.

"I also had to deal with my anger toward Paul. He knew he was drunk. He must have known that he shouldn't get in that car. And he left me as the only child of parents who haven't been able to cope since the day he died. They smother me now and worry about me all the time. I've been walking on eggs for years now, and I feel as if I'm losing my mind sometimes."

Karen and her family used their grief energy to pursue what they felt was injustice in punishing the driver who killed Paul. They met frustration after frustration and let it consume their lives. They became a dysfunctional family who could not resolve their grief and eventually accept Paul's untimely death. It is only now, five years later, that they are taking steps toward healing their lives—but at great expense. Karen lost five important years that could have been growthful for her.

Mothers Against Drunk Drivers (MADD) was founded in 1980 by Candy Lightner after her daughter Cari was killed by a drunk driver. She turned her grief energy into positive steps in pursuing stricter laws and punishments for drunk drivers.

MADD has grown into a nationwide movement that has publicized and promoted the need for change in our laws. It has succeeded in achieving major legislative changes.

MADD's progress includes:

- Passage of the National Minimum Drinking Age Act.
- Stiffer fines and jail sentences for driving while intoxicated.

According to Micky Sadoff, national president of MADD in 1989, the current goals of the organization are:

- Administrative revocation of drunk drivers' licenses in all fifty states. Currently only twenty-two states and the District of Columbia impose these sanctions, which are effective in reducing crashes.
- License plate confiscation for repeat offenders. Taking away a driver's license doesn't stop all repeat DUI offenders; no one knows that the driver is on revocation unless there is cause to check. Taking away license plates will be a strong deterrent because it is a visible revocation.
- Alcohol and drug testing of all drivers involved in motor vehicle accidents that cause death or serious injury.
- Funding of DUI enforcement programs by DUI offenders' fines.
- Jail sentences that cannot be suspended or commuted to probation.
- Restrictions on driving with open alcoholic beverage containers in cars.

The members of MADD from the president to the members working in your community are committed to making a difference. They fight to put an end to the drunk-driving tragedies that so many American families have had to endure.

Many of the MADD members have personally experienced the victimization and aftermath of drunk-driving accidents. Others are sickened by the violence erupting on the highways and streets of our country.

Micky Sadoff asked in an open letter recently, "Are you

aware that 25 percent of your auto insurance premiums goes toward paying the $24 billion that drunk drivers cost society each year in court costs, rehabilitation, and other expenses?"

CHAPTER ◇ 14

What Teens Can Do

MADD (Mothers Against Drunk Driving) was founded by Candy Lightner in 1980 after her teenage daughter, Cari Lightner, was killed by a drunk driver. Friends of Cari and her twin sister organized SADD (Students Against Driving Drunk) soon after. That was the beginning of teenagers becoming involved in the fight against the fatal combination of alcohol and driving.

Teens who are angered and sickened by the unnecessary and violent deaths of friends continue to organize groups to fight back against drunk drivers.

In 1981 another type of SADD was organized by Robert Anatas, who was then Director of Health Education in the Wayland Public Schools system in Massachusetts. Its goal was to keep teens from drinking and driving. The concept really took off.

You can begin a group. You can write to the national organization:

Students Against Driving Drunk
P.O. Box 800
Marlboro, MA 01752

SADD will send you information kits, parent contracts, and custom products to help you start your own chapter in your high school or town.

How do you get started?

Schedule an organization meeting and use the SADD Starter Kit. Invite friends, family, students, teachers, administrators, community officials, and everyone in your area to this first meeting. Invite speakers from other SADD groups, the governor's office, insurance companies, and others who are anti-driving drunk. By contacting the national SADD, you might be able to schedule Robert Anatas or another national speaker.

Be ready to dedicate hours of your own time to the cause. It takes a committed effort using a key group of hard workers like yourself to accomplish anything. Educate your friends and schoolmates about why this kind of group is needed. Get the okay from school officials, your principal, and superintendent. Tell them you want to work toward lowering the injury and death rate statistics from drunk driving.

Target a certain time of the year to begin a campaign. Talk to editors of your local newspaper and your school paper. Get community leaders involved. Have classmates sign petitions, or have sign-up drives for members. Get permission to teach younger grades about driving drunk or to put on skits for elementary school kids about the dangers of alcohol. (Kids are drinking younger and younger these days.)

Goals of your group:

1. Education about the dangers of drinking and driving.
2. Prevention—teaching ways kids can reduce their risks.

3. Action to change "the system" (government and laws) to protect people from drunk drivers.
4. Projects aimed at informational promotion and self-protection during prom and graduation times.

Appear on local cable TV. Solicit donations from local car companies or insurance groups for your expenses. Sell T-shirts, give away bumper stickers, info flyers, buttons, leaflets.

Hold bake sales, car washes, and fund drives to offset costs of materials.

Most work doesn't cost money. Your aim is to spread the word: DON'T DRINK AND DRIVE—SAVE LIVES.

FRIENDS DON'T LET FRIENDS DRIVE DRUNK.

SAFE

Many schools around the country are inaugurating SAFE programs. SAFE stands for Substance Abuse-Free Environment. The kids run promotional compaigns about staying straight and safe in situations where alcohol or drugs threaten the well-being of kids. SAFE operates on the local, state, and national levels.

Ann Marie Donegan, a junior in New Jersey, has been a motivating force behind her school's SAFE program.

"We work for SAFE in our schools to promote Project Graduation. Our advisor and our group arrange for announcements, stay-sober sign-ups, and many other activities to make kids aware that they don't have to drink to have a good time," Ann Marie said.

Ann Marie has also been a participant and trainer for the past two summers for TIGS (Teen Institute of the Garden State). This is an offshoot of the National Teen

Institute, a program urging that kids get "high on life" as an alternative to getting high on alcohol or drugs.

"I started as a participant and now am a trainer. Our work is based on team planning for general workshops followed by mini workshops. The team planning centers around solving problems in school and with kids. It's not only about alcohol and drugs. It teaches me more about myself and my community. *You be you* is a theme. You can get psyched up about not using and just being yourself."

Ann Marie's participation in TIGS overflows into her activities with her local and county SAFE projects.

"It's great to see other kids from the summer TIGS programs all year long. We all work together on Project Graduation, and the network that we've formed is strong. That's the important part—a network of kids who get high on life."

SAFE RIDES FOR TEENS

"Our big promotion this year is Safe Rides for Teens," explained Mary Beth of Florida. "Our high school chapter of SADD is organizing and operating a program that gives rides home to kids who have found themselves not wanting to drive with someone who was high.

"Mainly we man the phones for our call-in hotline number, and a volunteer parent or teacher and a student are on call on the weekends to pick up kids who call in."

Mary Beth said that some of the kids they pick up are not really in trouble. "They just want a ride somewhere. It's hard to make that kind of judgment call. I mean, if they call the hot line we should help them out. I'd hate to decide that someone didn't really need a ride and then find out the next day that they had been in an accident with a drunk driver."

There's a lot of setting up to do for Safe Rides and some liability involved, so you'll need help and supervision. Enlisting the aid of a local service organization may get you off to a good start.

Holiday weekends, proms, graduations, and parties are important times to offer Safe Rides. Some communities plan for Friday and Saturday nights from 10 pm to 3 am. Using CBs and telephones, parents and other adults in the community can be involved. It is a good idea to drive in teams of two or three. Keep records of picked-up kids, times, addresses. Set up guidelines for confidentiality; use seatbelts and large safe cars.

PROJECT GRADUATION

This is a national alcohol and safety program to keep kids safe during prom and graduation time.

Get your Student Council involved if you have no other organization in school to monitor and promote this worthwhile project.

1. Give information over the school PA system.
2. Have kids sign pledges not to drink and drive or get in a car with a drinking driver.
3. Set up a Safe Ride system.
4. Promote a "Buckle-Up Day."
5. Make posters of slogans repeating the message for Project Graduation: Stay alive, don't drink and drive.

SCARED STIFF

This is a hard-hitting program aimed at helping kids realize the frightening things that can happen to them when they are using, boozing, and driving. Write to:

Safety and Survival Inc.
P.O. Box 8305
Rockville, MD 20856

PARENT TAXIS

Set up parent pacts with several families. Maybe your best friend's father is willing to be on duty this weekend for your friends in case a safe ride is needed after a party or a concert. Next weekend could be your mother's and older brother's turn. Most families are glad to work out this kind of arrangement if you kids ask and set up some guidelines beforehand. It sure beats having your mom and dad sit up until four in the morning wondering where you are because your date passed out and you were stuck.

RENT-A-LIMO

When figuring out the expenses for the senior prom, many families add in the cost of renting a limousine.

"My girlfriend's father said he'd chip in half the cost of a limo for our prom," said, Michael, eighteen.

"He said he didn't want to have to worry about where we were and who was driving or what shape the driver was in. So we three couples shared the rest of the cost and went in style in a decked-out black limo. It was outasite!"

RADIO AND MEDIA ANNOUNCEMENTS

Public service information is in demand. Do radio and local cable TV announcements about staying straight, staying alive, buckling up, don't drink and drive, etc. When teens pose a responsible pitch to the local media, they can usually get on the air or on TV. Kids helping kids will make news.

CONTESTS

Run poster and slogan contests in the elementary and junior high schools in your town. Solicit local businesses to donate prizes (free pizza, movie tickets, two hours of roller skating at the rink, etc.) to entice the younger kids to make a statement and commitment to staying straight and off the booze.

Make sure you have things organized before you try to sell this idea to your school superintendent and principal. Presenting a responsible, organized plan will earn you respect and the green light to go ahead with these projects.

MEDIA CAMPAIGNS

Get a movement going in your school by having parents, teachers, administrators, and teens write letters and send petitions to the elected officials and judges in your community. Work to get the names of drunk drivers published in the newspaper. This has proved to be a successful campaign in some towns because kids and adults become a little more cautious if their "secret" of a drunk-driving arrest and license revocation may get out.

TV APPEARANCES

Get your act together and take it on the road on radio and cable TV talk shows. If you have a successful program going, spread the word! Others will join a popular cause, and it may save a life.

ORGANIZE A RALLY

Organize a large rally or assembly where speakers are people who have had harrowing experiences, or schoolmates who have lost a friend or relative in a drunk-driving crash. Plan for the local police or safety commission to do a car crash demonstration. Have a persuasive speaker who can get kids to take a pledge to stand up for their own lives and the right to be safe. Get newspaper coverage of the event.

"Our high school brought in all these semifamous sports people, mostly pro football and basketball players that some of us had heard about," said Kevin, fifteen. "They did a lot of talking with the athletes and in the health classes about staying straight. Some of them admitted to drinking and using, but they made it sound really bad. I think kids listened."

POSITIVE PEER PROGRAMS OR PEER COUNSELING

Kids helping kids. Students are used as role models, facilitators, helpers, and leaders. These teens are mentors to younger students who want information, help, a contact, or a good influence to deal with the daily stresses of adolescence. Peer counselors can target specific programs, especially with drinking and driving.

Some kids feel that they have no power, that they could never "change the world." But you can. Working on a SADD organization, helping kids get safe rides, promoting healthy habits to younger kids can all make a difference.

It can save a life, iincluding your own. Are you willing to invest some time in that?

CHAPTER ◇ 15

Pam Pays Forever

"I live in a small town where everybody knows everybody. No one's business is their own," said Pam, eighteen.

"I had a great group of friends, and the only problem was that there wasn't much to do in our town. If we wanted to go to the mall or the movies, we had to drive a half hour or more. So we'd drink as we drove. That way when we got where we were going we were high, feeling pretty good, and could have some fun.

"I never thought I was an alcoholic. I mean, teenagers aren't really alcoholics. All kids drink. Show me one kid who never drinks and I'll show you someone who has no friends, because friends are where it's at. Being with my friends was even more important most of the time than being with my parents. If you want friends, you do all the same things together because that's the way things are.

"Grown-ups push things at us like, 'You shouldn't hang around with that crowd' or 'You have to change your friends'. Be real. Especially in a small town like mine, that will never happen.

"Anyway, my friends and I would drink when we went

anywhere. We started like about fourteen or fifteen when we could get someone's older brother or sister to get us stuff and drive us around. But it really got better when we all started driving. Then we could get out of town fast and start partying.

"We would party as soon as we left school. I can't tell you how many nights I went home drunk, ate dinner with my family, did my homework, and then crashed. The next day I'd look at my homework and have to laugh at how sloppy it was.

"My parents never said anything to me. Either they didn't see it because they were so busy, or they pretended it wasn't real. Maybe that was it. I don't know. My teachers never suspected. I mean, we didn't drink in school. We were good students, got decent grades, were well liked. I was even vice-president of my class, get that! So nobody knew. That's what made it so much better. My friends and I had like this secret society that no one else was a part of, especially parents and teachers. It was great, we all thought.

"Anyway, one night after an especially good party I was driving everyone home. We had seatbelts on. See, we listen to all that health and driver ed stuff in school. My friend Steffi lives on this neat hill and you have to do a sharp downhill turn to get into her driveway.

"This night I must have been going a little too fast plus I was pretty high. I skidded into her driveway and it was kinda dark. Everything happened so fast, it seems now like it was a video or something.

"When I pulled into Steffi's driveway, her father and little brother must have just gotten home. Ricky was crossing in back of their car to go into the house when I rammed into their car from the back. Oh, God! It was horrible!"

Pam stopped, too choked up to speak. It took a few minutes for her composure to return and for her to continue.

"Ricky was wedged between my car and theirs. Steffi's father had been right outside and saw the whole thing. Steffi was in my back seat and didn't know what happened right away. Then when she saw Ricky there she started screaming and screaming. That's all I remember—Steffi screaming and screaming.

"There were police cars and an ambulance, flashing lights, people crying. I remember the policeman asking me questions like about how much I had been drinking. . .

"The next thing I remember is sitting in this room at the police station and looking at this clock. You know, like the ones we have in school—the institutional kind. And the clock said 12:00 midnight. Two hours earlier I had been having fun with my friends, and now I was in the police station being questioned. I had already had blood tests at the hospital emergency room and breath tests too.

"I kept thinking that this was just a dream, a bad dream, a nightmare. I'm gonna wake up soon and Ricky won't be in the hospital because I smashed him with my car. I was worried that Steffi would be mad at me. Could you imagine that? I didn't want her mad at me for hurting her brother. I was afraid that I had hurt him bad. Then everyone would be mad at me. Here I was without a scratch, and Ricky was in the emergency room.

"You see, Ricky was this great athlete. Even though he was only in eighth grade, he was the star of the Pop Warner football team and on the school basketball team. All the coaches in our high school were dying for Ricky to get to high school so they could have a great team. He was that good.

"People even used to joke about a scholarship to UCLA

or Notre Dame. Stuff like that. And now I had put him in the hospital. The whole town would hate me. Why hadn't I been more careful? All I shoulda done was drive slower or hit the brakes faster. It never occurred me at the time how drunk I really was and that I probably couldn't get to the brakes any faster.

"The policeman said my parents were waiting for me outside. I didn't want to see them. They were probably mad at me too. I could just imagine my stepfather. He and I didn't get along anyway, plus I had crashed up his car. But I was surprised when I saw them. My mother was crying and my stepfather was pale, like stunned or something.

"My mother came over to me. I was still a little out of it. Shock, I guess, or maybe the booze I drank, and she told me that Ricky had died at the hospital. I think I went a little crazy at that point. I screamed something like 'NO! NO! He's not dead!' Not Ricky. He was only thirteen. I didn't kill him. God, it sounded like murder or something.

"Now that I look back, it *was* murder. I had killed him. I was drunk and I was driving and I killed him. If I could have died right then and there, I would have.

"I thought a lot about killing myself over the next few days. I mean, if Ricky was dead, what right did I have to be alive? He didn't deserve it. He was a kid. My best friend's little brother. I think my mother must have been told to watch me, because she kept coming to my room to check on me.

"I couldn't leave my room. I felt paralyzed. I wished I was paralyzed, then at least people would say, 'Oh, poor Pam. It was an accident. Ricky's dead and she'll never walk again. Poor girl.' Would that make us even, Rick? Somehow I don't think so.

"My parents went to Ricky's funeral, and they left my

aunt to stay with me. I snuck into their room and got the gun that my stepfather kept in his closet. But I couldn't find any bullets. Damn, how could they do this to me? They hid the bullets! I tore that room apart looking for the bullets. I really wanted to die that day.

My aunt found me screaming and crying about the bullets, ripping apart my parents' bedroom. She grabbed me and held on. I was out of control and crying. She held on and hugged me and hugged me and told me she didn't want me to die—that I could make it even after what had happened.

"I guess I needed that shred of hope—that I could go on and live even though Ricky was dead. But how? I couldn't live in this town anymore. I couldn't face Steffi and her parents. I couldn't go back to school. I thought about running away. Running far away to a place where no one knew my name. Cut my hair and be a different person. I wanted to run away from what I had done.

"During those first few days I also wanted a drink. Bad. I stayed in my room and I wanted to get drunk. Then I wouldn't have to face things. But you know what? Even then I didn't think I had an alcohol problem. It was an accident. Steffi could have been driving instead of me, right?

"My parents argued a lot that first week. My stepfather was angry and embarrassed. I guess I don't blame him now, but then it gave me an excuse to hate him. I hated myself so much that it came natural to hate him too. My mother cried a lot, but she stuck by me. She and my aunt, her sister, were the only ones who stuck by me.

"No one called me except the police and lawyers and those kinds of people. But not my friends. Funny thing was, I thought some of them would call. Not Steffi, but maybe Janice or Mandy. But no one did. I guess I wanted some sympathy. I mean, it was a terrible thing to happen to me too...

"I wasn't going back to school. I was going to live in my room forever or run away. I never wanted to see anybody in this town again. But my stepfather made me. Even my mother said I should face things. I hated them for that.

"They drove me to school that first day. No one talked to me. The kids moved away when I walked down the hall to my locker, you know like in those old movies where someone had a disease and no one wants to be near him? That's what happened. My counselor talked to me, and a few teachers, but I think that no one knew what to do with me.

"I only got through part of the day, sick to my stomach. I cut out early and went home. I never wanted to go back there again. As soon as I got home and found that the house was empty, I started drinking. I drank almost the whole bottle of vodka that my stepfather keeps for company. And I drank it down in an hour and a half. I puked up a lot of it, and my mother found me passed out on the bathroom floor when she came home from work early.

"I remember waking up in the hospital and crying. I couldn't stop crying. I wanted to be dead and I wasn't. I couldn't face my life or myself anymore.

"There was this counselor at the hospital who talked to me. Maybe I was ready for help or maybe she was just this magic person, but she helped me realize that I needed help. Help with my alcohol addiction, help with my suicide attempts, help to face life.

"I joined Alcoholics Anonymous. The AA program was part of what saved my life. Another part was the counseling I got, but it wasn't easy. Facing my problems, going back to school, admitting I was an alcoholic were only the first steps.

"What I found out, though, was that there were people who cared about me—and I was a drunk, a murderer, a no-good. It was hard to believe that these other people wanted to help me live. I didn't think I was worth it for a long time.

"One day at school, after some kids put a note in my locker with 'KID KILLER' on it, I found another note. I wasn't even going to open it, but I did.

"The note said, 'I know you're going through a hard time, but if you need a friend, maybe I can help.' It was signed by a girl I used to make fun of. But you know, I really needed a friend, and to think that she'd gone out of her way to send me that note felt real good. So I did make friends with her and she turned out to be real nice. It felt good to have a friend again.

"It's almost a year and a half since I killed Ricky. I'm graduating soon, even going on to business school. Steffi has never forgiven me or even talked to me, and I don't really expect her to. My parents got divorced. I think all of this was too much for my stepfather to take. My mother stuck by me, but she looks a lot older and sadder now.

"I had to go to court for my crime, and I lost my license for a long time. We had to scrape up money to pay for the fines and lawyer's fees. The judge sentenced me to community work every weekend for six months. I spent time helping out in the hospital emergency room and on the children's floor. That was hard. I kept seeing Ricky's face and messing up.

"I keep on going to AA meetings, sometimes every night, and on weekends too. I wanted to drink a lot of times, but I wanted to get better too, and I can't do both at the same time.

"Getting drunk and driving that night and killing Ricky is something I live with twenty-four hours a day. It'll never go away. If anyone had ever told me that this would happen, I wouldn't have believed it.

"Kids don't believe things like that. They'll go out and do it anyway. This weekend there'll still be kids in town drunk all over the place and driving around in cars. And they could end up like me—killing someone...and paying the price forever..."

Opinion Survey

Do this survey again. See if your opinions remain the same.

Directions: To indicate your feelings about each statement accurately, mark the following in the blanks.

D—strongly disagree
d —moderately disagree
? —unsure
a —moderately agree
A—strongly agree.

1. Driving home from a party after you've been drinking is very dangerous. ____
2. Some people drive more cautiously after they've been drinking. ____
3. If someone you hardly know at a party wants to drive drunk, it's really none of your business. ____
4. Teenagers have more accidents after drinking than adults. ____
5. Alcohol starts affecting you as soon as it is swallowed. ____
6. The odds of being in an alcohol-related accident in your life are very small. ____
7. Teens convicted of drunk driving should receive less severe punishment than adult offenders. ____
8. Fifty percent of fatal traffic accidents involve alcohol. ____

9. A few wine coolers can't make you drunk enough to have difficulty driving. ____
10. Alcohol is absorbed into your bloodstream very slowly. ____
11. Drinking two cups of strong coffee can sober you up enough to drive safely after drinking. ____
12. When you drink two 12-ounce cans of beer, it takes one hour for the alcohol to leave your body so it is safe to drive. ____
13. The chances of being caught driving drunk are small enough that it's okay to be a little high when you are behind the wheel. ____
14. The advertisements of alcohol and beer companies are harmless and don't really influence teens to drink. ____
15. The alcohol of choice for most teenagers is beer. ____
16. Most police officers will let you off with a warning if they stop you for driving while intoxicated, especially if it is your first time. ____
17. Judges go easy on teen first-time offenders for drunk driving. ____
18. Some drivers drive better after a few drinks. ____
19. It takes a lot of drinks for the alcohol level in your blood to reach .10, the legal limit for intoxicated drivers. ____

Appendix

ADDRESSES, INFORMATION, AND RESOURCES

You can write to the following organizations for material on drinking and driving:

Al-Anon Family Group Headquarters, Inc.
P.O. Box 182, Madison Square Station
New York, NY 10159-0182

Alateen
P.O. Box 182, Madison Square Station
New York, NY 10159-0182

Alcohol and Drug Problems Association of North America, Inc. (ADPA)
444 North Capital Street NW
Washington, DC 20001

Alcoholics Anonymous World Services, Inc.
P.O. Box 459, Grand Central Station
New York, NY 10163

Citizens for Safe Drivers Against Drunk Drivers and Other Chronic Offenders
P.O. Box 42018
Washington, DC 20015

Highway Users Foundation
1776 Massachusetts Avenue, NW
Washington, DC 20036

Insurance Institute for Highway Safety
Watergate 600
Washington, DC 20037

Mothers Against Drunk Drivers (MADD)
669 Airport Freeway
Hurst, TX 76052

National Clearinghouse for Alcohol Information
U.S. Department of Health and Human Services
P.O. Box 2345
Rockville, MD 20852

National Commission Against Drunk Drivers
1705 DeSale Street NW
Washington, DC 20036

National Highway Traffic Safety Administration
400 Seventh Street SW
Washington, DC 20590

National Institute on Alcohol Abuse and Alcoholism
Parklawn Building
5600 Fishers Lane
Rockville, Md 20857

National Safety Council
444 North Michigan Avenue
Chicago, IL 60611

Remove Intoxicated Drivers (RID)
P.O. Box 520
Schenectedy, NY 12301

Students Against Driving Drunk (SADD)
P.O. Box 800
Marlboro, MA 01752

American Automobile Association
8111 Gatehouse Road
Falls Church, VA 22047

PLACES TO GO FOR INFORMATION

State Department of Transportation

County Department of Transportation

Local Police Department

State Police Department

Local Court System

County Court System

State Court System

Local, county, and state public health department

Your own insurance company

Local chapters of Alcoholics Anonymous (AA), Alateen, and Al-Anon

(Most of the above addresses and telephone numbers are in your phone book.)

Bibliography

BOOKS

American Automobile Association. *Teacher's Guide to Alcohol Countermeasures.* Falls Church, Virginia, 1976.

Fishman, Ross, PhD. *Alcohol and Alcoholism, The Encyclopedia of Psychoactive Drugs.* New York: Chelsea House Publishers, 1986.

Howard, Marion. *Did I Have a Good Time?* New York: Continuum Publishing Corporation, 1980.

Golden, Sandy. *Driving the Drunk Off the Road.* Gaithersburg, MD: Quince Mill Books, 1983.

Milgram, Gail Gleason. *Coping with Alcohol.* New York: Rosen Publishing Group, Inc., 1985.

Newman, Susan. *You Can Say No to a Drink or a Drug—What Every Kid Should Know.* New York: Putnam Publishing Group, Perigee Books, 1986.

Stearn, Marshall B., PhD. *Drinking and Driving, Know Your Limits and Liabilities.* Sausalito, CA: Park West Publishing Co., 1985.

PAMPHLETS

AAA Traffic Safety Department. "Alcohol, Vision, and Driving." Falls Church, Virginia, 1975.

———. "Drunk Driving: Is There an Answer?" Falls Church, Virginia, 1987.

Fleming, Anne, ed. "Teenage Drivers." Washington, DC Insurance Institute for Highway Safety: 1987.

Highway Users Federation. "Programs to Reduce Alcohol and

Other Drug-impaired Driving. Washington, DC, 1988.
Insurance Institute for Highway Safety." Fatal Crash Involvement and Laws Against Alcohol-impaired Driving." Arlington, Virginia, 1988.
———. "Alcohol." Washington, DC, 1987.
Malfetti, Dr. James L. "DWI Countermeasures, "Falls Church, VA: AAA Traffic Safety Department, 1982.
Milgram, Dr. Gail. "What Is Alcohol and Why Do People Drink?" New Brunswick, NJ: Center of Alcohol Studies, Rutgers University, 1988.
National Commission Against Drunk Driving. "Youth Driving Without Impairment." Washington, DC, 1988.
National Highway Traffic Safety Administration. "Alcohol Involvement in Fatal Traffic Crashes 1987." Washington, DC, 1988.
———. "Consensus Report on Impaired Driving." Washington, DC, 1989.
———. "Drunk Driving Facts." Washington, DC, 1988.
National Institute on Alcohol Abuse and Alcoholism, National Highway Traffic Safety Administration. "Together We Can Prevent Alcohol-impaired Driving," Washington, DC, 1984.
U.S. Department of Health and Human Services, National Institute on Drug Abuse. "Effects of Drugs on Driving." Washington, DC, 1985.
National Safety Council. "Will You Make It Home Tonight?" Chicago, Illinois, 1984.
———. "The Designated Driver: Being a Friend," Chicago, Illinois, 1985.

Index